T0196060

The King is Coming!

A Bible Study of Revelation for This Generation

Elizabeth Smith

WESTBOW
PRESS°

A DIVISION OF THOMAS NELSON
& ZONDERVAN

WestBow Press books may be ordered through booksellers or by contacting:

WestBow Press
A Division of Thomas Nelson & Zondervan
1663 Liberty Drive
Bloomington, IN 47403
www.westbowpress.com
1 (866) 928-1240

Interior Image Credit: Kailyn Gerringer

All Scripture quotations are taken from the King James Version.

ISBN: 978-1-9736-8955-3 (sc)
ISBN: 978-1-9736-8954-6 (e)

Print information available on the last page.

WestBow Press rev. date: 4/6/2020

This book is dedicated first to the Lord Jesus for giving me the comfort of Revelation in a lonely time in my life; to my wise husband Eric who helped me in many conversations to develop the understanding of this Scripture; to my daughters Amber and Tegan and their husbands Joseph and Dirk and my grandchildren Penelope, John Judah and Trip, who taught me the value of listening and learning the lessons of God; and lastly, many thanks to the test groups who have gone through this study helping me edit the material.

HELPFUL HINTS AS YOU STUDY REVELATION

This is not an exhaustive cross reference study of the Book of Revelation. It is a thoughtful study which will hopefully excite you about our coming King Jesus enough to dig into scripture and find many cross references to answer your questions.

Before you begin this study every week pray and ask the Holy Spirit to lead you into all truth. John 16:13 says, "Howbeit when he, the Spirit of truth, is come, he will guide you into all truth: for he shall not speak of himself; but whatsoever he shall hear, that shall he speak: and he will shew you things to come." King James Bible (may be referred to as 'KJV'.)

All of the following terms refer to the last book in the Bible called "Revelation", "The Revelation", "Book of Revelation".

This study is done with The King James Ryrie Study Bible Version as it's reference. As a result of this some of the other translations may use different words for ideas referenced. (Example: Revelation chapter 5:1 reads 'a book' which in other versions of the Bible may be read as 'scroll').

"Ch." means chapter.

"Vs." means verse.

When reading a chapter and verse in the Bible it is listed as follows: Revelation 4:5 which means Revelation chapter four and verse five.

We consider all the writing, description and word pictures in the Book of Revelation as literal. These things occurred as they are written in other words. If you have trouble with this, imagine for just a moment the apostle John an author from 2,000 years ago, trying to describe what he is seeing.

Contents

REVELATION CHAPTER 1 1

REVELATION CHAPTERS 2 AND 3 7

REVELATION CHAPTER 4 13

REVELATION CHAPTER 5 19

REVELATION CHAPTERS 6 AND 7 25

REVELATION CHAPTER 8 31

REVELATION CHAPTER 9 35

REVELATION CHAPTERS 10 AND 11 41

REVELATION CHAPTER 12 49

REVELATION CHAPTER 13 55

REVELATION CHAPTER 14 61

REVELATION CHAPTERS 15 AND 16 65

REVELATION CHAPTERS 17 AND 18 71

REVELATION CHAPTERS 19 AND 20 77

REVELATION CHAPTERS 21 AND 22 83

REVELATION CHAPTER 1

OVERVIEW FOR IN-CLASS FILL IN

WEEK 1

1. What is the meaning of the word "revelation"? (Use any source)
2. Who is the author of the book of Revelation according to the Revelation 1:1?
3. What is the date the Revelation was written? (FROM ANY SOURCE)

HINT: THE ENTIRE BOOK OF REVELATION IS ABOUT THE REVELATION OF JESUS

4. In a few words from your Bible give a brief outline of the book of Revelation:

Chapter1 _____

Chapter 2-3 _____

Chapter 4-5 _____

Chapter 6-19:1-10 _____

Chapter 19:11-21 _____

Chapter 20 _____

Chapter 21 _____

5. Complete the phrase which lists the broad outline in chapter 1:19 below.

The things ... (chapter 1):

The things … (chapters 2-3):

The things … (chapters 4-22):

REVELATION CHAPTER 1:1-9

Read the following verses and answer the questions.

6. **(vs.1) The who**-Who is the Revelation about?
7. **(vs.2) The how**-How is the Revelation presented?
8. **(vs.3) The why**- Why is it important to read the Revelation?
9. **(vs.3)** How can one be blessed?
10. **(vs.4)** To whom is John writing?
11. **(vs.4)** Complete the 3-fold greeting? Grace be unto you, and peace, from him…

    1.   2.   3.

12. Name the seven churches in chapters 2 and 3.

    1.   2.   3.   4.   5.   6.   7.

13. The number seven occurs 54 times in the book of Revelation. Write examples of the number seven as you look through the first three chapters of Revelation.
14. Do you have any ideas of the prophetic meaning of the number seven?
15. **(vs.4)** Who is sending the greeting "grace and peace"?
16. **(vs.5)** Who is the second greeter and what are his descriptors?

    1.   2.   3.   4.

17. **(vs.6)** How should believers in Christ view their position while reading Revelation?

    Why?

18. **(vs.7)** What is the great Revelation?
19. **(vs.7)** What is the 2-fold purpose of Revelation?
20. Who is named as The Alpha and the Omega (The first and the last) in each selection below?

    John 1:1-3

    Colossians 1:13-17

    Hebrews 1:1-4

    Ephesians 1: 3-10

I. THE REVELATION EXPERIENCE: "THE THINGS WHICH THOU HAST SEEN" 1:10-20

HINT: THIS IS OUR PRACTICAL TRIBULATION MANUAL TO REMEMBER DAILY!

21. **(vs.9-10)** What are we to remember and how are we to act in tribulation?
22. **(vs.11)** Who made an announcement in a way John could understand?
23. Why was this announcement made?
24. **(vs.12)** What are the 7 candlesticks? (Also explained in verse 20)?
25. **(vs.13)** Who is in the midst of the candlesticks?
26. Who claims to be "the Light of the world" in John 8:12?

JESUS DESCRIBED 1:13B-16

27. **(vs.13b)** How is the son of man dressed?
28. Why are we told about his golden sash/girdle? See Exodus 28:4.
29. **(vs.14)** Describe his head and hair. Read Daniel 7:9.
30. What does this signify? Read Isaiah 1:18.
31. **(vs.14)** Describe his eyes.
32. Read Malachi 3:2-3 and tell what is said about the refiner's fire.
33. **(vs.15)** Describe his feet.
34. What might brass be significant of? Read Daniel 2:39.
35. **(vs.15)** Describe his voice.
36. What does Isaiah 12:2-3 say about water?
37. **(vs.16)** What is in his right hand and what does verse 20 say about this?
38. **(vs.16)** What came out of his mouth?
39. What does Ephesians 6:17 say about the sword?
40. **(vs.16)** Describe his countenance?
41. What does Matthew 17:2 say about Jesus' countenance?

RESPONSE AND DIRECTIONS 1:17-20

42. **(vs.17)** What was John's response to seeing the son of man?
43. **(vs.17)** What was Jesus' response to John?
44. In Matthew 17:6, what was the disciple's response to hearing God's voice at Jesus' transfiguration?
45. What was Jesus' response to the disciples?
46. **(vs.18)** Jesus shows his authority and gives what message of hope for John and all believers?
47. **(vs.18)** What keys does Jesus have?
48. What does Revelation 20:14 say is the ultimate end of hell and death?
49. **(vs.19)** What are John's directions from Jesus?
50. **(vs.20)** What are the 7 stars?

51. **(vs.21)** What are the 7 gold candlesticks?

Chapter one is now behind you and you are blessed. Continue to chapter two.

SPOILER: Here is the church, here is the steeple, open the doors and see all the people!

NOTES OR OTHER REFERENCES

REVELATION CHAPTER 1 ANSWER KEY

1. The revealing or unveiling
2. John
3. 64AD or 81-95AD.
4. Chapter 1 Christ revealed in his glory

   Chapter 2-3 Description of and instruction to the 7 churches

   Chapter 4-5 The lamb slain and risen, worship direction

   Chapter 6-19:1-10 The lamb shows wrath, 7 year tribulation

   Chapter 19:11-21 Christ returns

   Chapter 20 Jesus as millennial ruler and king

   Chapter 21 The Triune God in the new heaven and earth

5. John saw (Chapter 1)

   Which are (Chapter 2-3)

   Which shall be (Chapter 4-22)

6. God, Jesus, Holy Spirit (believer's and non-believers but the focus of revelation is the triune God)
7. It is presented as a record of John's true vision of what he saw, the present and the future
8. There is a blessing attached to reading Revelation
9. Blessing comes from reading Revelation and hearing the word of the prophecy
10. He is writing To the 7 churches in Asia
11. 1. which is 2.which was 3.which is to come
12. 1. Ephesus 2. Smyrna 3. Pergamum 4. Thyatyra 5. Sardis 6. Philadelphia 7. Laodicia
13. Dooms, New things, Churches, Lampstands, Stars, Seals, Scrolls, Hours, Eyes of the Lamb, Angels, Trumpets, Spirits, Thunders, Heads of the dragon, Golden bowls, Kings
14. Seven comes after 6 and before 8; it is important in the Book of Revelation and is connected to God or represents him in a mysterious way
15. 1. John 2. God 3. Seven spirits before his throne 4. Jesus the Christ
16. 1. Faithful witness 2. Firstborn of the dead 3. Ruler of the kings of the earth 4. He who washed our sins by his blood
17. We are a kingdom, priests to his God and Father. The glory and dominion are his forever and ever
18. Jesus is coming in the clouds
19. Everyone will see him including those who pierced him, All the families of the earth will mourn over him

20. John 1:1- the Word (Christ)
    Colossians 1:13-17 - God's son

    Hebrews 1:1-4 - God's son

    Ephesians 1:3-11 - God, Christ

21. We are to remember we have brothers in tribulation, We are not alone, We are to act patiently and live in the Spirit
22. The Alpha and Omega made an announcement
23. John was to write it in a book and send it to the 7 churches (and ultimately to all believers)
24. They are the 7 churches
25. One like the Son of man
26. Jesus
27. He is wearing a long robe to his feet and a golden girdle around his waist
28. It refers to Jesus as high priest
29. White like wool, as white as snow
30. Signifies Christ's forgiveness of our sin by purification
31. His eyes were as flames of fire
32. It is a cleanser and will purify and purge
33. His feet were like fine brass burned in a furnace
34. Rulership or kingdoms
35. Like the sound of many waters
36. Water comes from wells of salvation
37. Seven stars, The 7 stars are the angels of the 7 churches
38. A sharp two-edged sword
39. The sword of the Spirit is the Word of God
40. His countenance was as a bright sunshine
41. He was transfigured and his face shone like the sun
42. John fell at his feet like he was dead
43. Jesus laid his right hand on him and said, "Don't be afraid"
44. They fell on their faces and were very afraid
45. "Get up. Don't be afraid."
46. Jesus says he is the one who lives and was dead and is alive forever
47. He has the keys to hell and death
48. Death and hell are cast into the lake of fire as the second death
49. Write the things he saw, the things which are and the things which shall be
50. The seven stars are the angels of the 7 churches
51. The seven gold candlesticks are the 7 churches

REVELATION CHAPTERS 2 AND 3

THE SEVEN CHURCHES -
"THE THINGS WHICH ARE"

WEEK 2

Answer the following questions about each church.

1. **EPHESUS (2:1-7)**
   To whom is this written?
   Description of he who says these things:
   What does he "know"?
   What does he have "against" them?
   What will he do?
   What is his encouragement?
   What is his promise?
   What is the final admonition from him?

2. **SMYRNA (2:8-11)**
   To whom is this written?
   Description of he who says these things:
   What does he "know"?
   What does he have "against" them?
   What will he do?
   What is his encouragement?
   What is his promise?
   What is the final admonition from him?

3. **PERGAMUM (2:12-17)**
   To whom is this written?
   Description of he who says these things:

What does he "know"?
What does he have "against" them?
What will he do?
What is his encouragement?
What is his promise?
What is the final admonition from him?

4. **THYATIRA (2:18-29)**
   To whom is this written?
   Description of he who says these things:
   What does he "know"?
   What does he have "against" them?
   What will he do?
   What is his encouragement?
   What is his promise?
   What is the final admonition from him?

5. **SARDIS (3:1-6)**
   To whom is this written?
   Description of he who says these things:
   What does he "know"?
   What does he have "against" them?
   What will he do?
   What is his encouragement?
   What is his promise?
   What is the final admonition from him?

6. **PHILADELPHIA (3:7-13)**
   To whom is this written?
   Description of he who says these things:
   What does he "know"?
   What does he have "against" them?
   What will he do?
   What is his encouragement?
   What is his promise?
   What is the final admonition from him?

7. **LAODICEA (3:14-22)**
   To whom is this written?
   Description of he who says these things:
   What does he "know"?
   What does he have "against" them?

What will he do?
What is his encouragement?
What is his promise?
What is the final admonition from him?

SPOILER: Doors to heaven are about to open as you read the next chapter in Revelation!

NOTES OR OTHER REFERENCES

REVELATION CHAPTERS 2 AND 3 ANSWER KEY

1. **Ephesis**

   Who- Angel of the church of Ephesus.

   Description- Holds seven stars in his right hand, walks in the midst of the seven golden candlesticks (Jesus – Revelation 1:20).

   Know- Their works, labor, patience, can't bear evil ones, tried some apostles and found them liars, persevered with patience, labored for his name's sake and not become weary.

   Against- Have left first love (Matthew 24:12, Deuteronomy 6:5).

   Do- He will come quickly and remove their candlestick unless they repent.

   Encouragement- They hate the deeds of the Nicolaitanes as he does (a sect which took license in Christian conduct- Ryrie Study Bible note), they remember where they have fallen and repent, do the first works.

   Promise- Overcomers will be given to eat of the tree of life in the midst of the garden of God.

   Admonition- He who has an ear let him hear, through the Spirit what is said to the churches.

2. **Smyrna**-

   Who- Angel at the church of Smyrna.

   Description- He is the first and last, was dead and is now alive.

   Know- Their works, tribulation, poverty, blasphemy of people who say they are of Jesus but are actually of the church of Satan.

   Against- He has nothing against this church to pronounce.

   Do- Give a crown of life.

   Encouragement- Do not fear suffering for the devil will put some in prison for 10 days (Daniel 1:12-time chosen to prove the servants of God).

   Promise- He that overcomes will not be hurt in the second death (1 john 5:4-5).

   Admonition- He who has an ear let him hear, through the Spirit what is said to the churches.

3. **Pergamum**-

   Who- The angel of the church at Pergamum.

   Description- He who has a sharp two-edged sword (See Hebrews 4: 12).

   Know- Their works, where they live, where Satan's seat is, they hold fast his name and not denied the faith, that the martyr Antipas was killed among them where Satan dwells.

   Against- They hold to the doctrine of Balaam (Jude 11-Illgotten gain and dishonesty), and encourage others to sin (Nicolaitanes-see above in Ephesis).

   Do- He will come quickly and fight against them with the sword of his mouth.

   Encouragement- Repent.

   Promise- Overcomers will be given hidden manna (Exodus 16:31-33), a white stone with their new name on it which only the recipient will know.

   Admonition- He who has an ear let him hear, through the Spirit what is said to the churches.

4. **Thyatira**-

   Who- The angel of the church in Thyatira.

   Description- "Son of God", eyes like flames of fire (Daniel 10:6), feet like fine brass.

Know- Their works (said twice), charity, service, faith, patience, latter works are more than their first works (growth of service).

Against- They let Jezebel (1 Kings 16:31, 2 Kings 9) who labels herself a prophetess, teach and seduce his servants to fornicate (have sex between 2 married people out of wedlock), and eat idol-sacrificed food.

Do- Gave Jezebel time to repent (she didn't), cast her in a tribulation bed with her co-adulterers (unless they repent), will kill her children with death and all churches will know He is the one who searches the hearts giving according to their works.

Encouragement- Those who don't know the depths of Satan and this doctrine will have no other burden put on them.

Promise- The overcomer who keeps his works until the end will be given power over the nations to rule with a rod of iron (example of the potters work) as he received of his Father, he is given the Morning Star

Admonition- He who has an ear let him hear, through the Spirit what is said to the churches.

5. **Sardis-**

   Who- The angel of the church in Sardis.

   Description- The One who has the seven Spirits of God and seven stars (See Revelation 1:14-16).

   Know- Their works and their name, they are alive but are spiritually dead (See Matthew 23:27-28).

   Against- Has not found their works perfect before God.

   Do- Come on them when they are not watching as a thief and they won't know the hour (1 Thessalonians 4:16-17, 5:2).

   Encouragement- There are a few people who have not defiled their garments and will walk with Him in white for they are worthy (Psalm 51:7).

   Promise- He will not blot their name out of the Book of Life (Revelation 20:12-15) but will confess His name before the Father and His angels

   Admonition- He who has an ear let him hear, through the Spirit what is said to the churches.

6. **Philadelphia-**

   Who- The angel of the church in Philadelphia.

   Description- He is holy, true, has the key of David, He opens and no man shuts, shuts and no man opens.

   Know- Their works, has set before them an open door and no man can shut it, they have little strength but have kept His word and not denied His name.

   Against- Nothing.

   Do- Make them of Satan's synagogue who lie and say they are Jews, come and worship at their feet to know that He has loved them, keep them from the hour of temptation which will come on the whole earth to try earth dwellers.

   Encouragement- Hold onto what you have so that no man can take your crown.

   Promise- Overcomers will be a pillar in the temple of his God to remain forever, will write on him the name of God, the city of God (Jerusalem which will come down out of heaven), and write on him a new name.

   Admonition- He who has an ear let him hear, through the Spirit what is said to the churches.

7. **Laodicea-**

   Who- The angel of the church in Laodicea.

   Description- The faithful and true witness who is called the Amen, the beginning of the creation of God (John 1:1-5).

   Know- They are neither cold nor hot (He would rather they were one or the other).

   Against- They say they are rich having goods and need nothing but they don't know their spiritual condition (wretched, miserable, poor, blind, naked).

   Do- Counseled them to buy from Him fire-tested gold to be rich and white clothes to be clothed and not be naked, and eye ointment so they can see.

   Encouragement- Those He loves He rebukes and chastens, repent with zeal, He stands at the door and knocks.

   Promise- If anyone hears His voice and opens the door He will come in and eat with him, and that man will eat with Him, he that overcomes with be granted to sit with Him in His throne like He overcame and sat with His Father in His throne.

   Admonition- He who has an ear let him hear, through the Spirit what is said to the churches.

REVELATION CHAPTER 4

IN HEAVEN BEFORE THE START OF TRIBULATION "THE THINGS WHICH SHALL BE HEREAFTER"

WEEK 3

REFRESHER: Let's remember John's outline of Revelation 1:19. He tells us how the order of Revelation will be written: The things **which he has seen**, the things **which are** or the current events and the things or events **which have yet to occur.**

CHAPTER 4- introduction:

John writes with much symbolism in chapter 4 but the reality in our understanding of this should be greater than the symbolic. Chapter 4 leads us to the throne of God. As we consider heaven, always pay attention to color. We will learn about the One who will judge mankind. Remember the "churches" of Revelation 2-3? The word "church" is not mentioned again in the book of Revelation. There is a tabernacle in Ezekiel chapters 25-32 and 35-40. Read this at your leisure. It is a description or picture of heaven.

John's Vision

Read the following verses and answer the questions.

1. **(vs.1)** Through what does John enter heaven?

    Which churches in chapters 2 and 3 referred to the "door"?

    The trumpet voice may refer to what? See 1 Thessalonians 4:13-18.

    In what time frame does John put the vision?

2. **(vs.2)** What did John see with his spiritual eye?

    The throne was occupied by how many?

3. **(vs.3)** As what color stones did the One on the throne appear?

    In Exodus 39:1-14, who wore precious stones and what did he represent?

    What surrounded the throne to represent God's eternal commitment to man? Read Genesis 9:11-17.

4. **(vs.4)** The next thing John notices is how many lesser seats surrounding the throne of God?

    In 1 Chronicle 24:4, how many faithful priests of God are numbered?

    What might white robes symbolize in Revelation 6:11, 7:9?

    The Crowns of these elders represent what? Read Romans 8:17 and 2 Tim. 2:12.

5. **(vs.5)** Lightning and thundering and voices around the throne are similar to what other important event? Read Exodus 19:16-20, 20:18-19.

    The 7 spirits of God may represent what? Read Revelation 1:4, Isaiah 11:2.
    Revelation 4:5 shows the Holy Spirit is represented by the 7 lamps of fire. In Matthew 3:16 and Acts 2:3 the Holy Spirit is represented as what other 2 things?

6. **(vs.6)** What was before the throne?

    In 2 Corinthians 3:18, "beholding in a glass" represents what?

7. **(vs.7)** Describe the 4 living creatures around the throne.

8. **(vs.8)** What is their purpose? (For further understand of the creatures Read; Ezekiel 1:4-14 and 10:20-22.)

    Who are the beasts in Ezekiel 10:20-22?

In Revelation 1:8, the idea of threes is eternal. Which phrase shows us this?

9. **(vs.9)** What 3 praises do the beasts give him who sits on the throne?

10. **(vs.10)** In response to their call to worship, what do the 24 elders do?

    (Vs.9-10) What is another word we use for "forever and ever"?

    Elders credit God alone for the worthiness of their works by giving him what?

    (Vs.10-11) What is the purpose of our crowns?

11. **(vs.11)** All things were created for what purpose?

BELIEVER'S CROWNS

Read the references below and write your thoughts.

1. The crown of life- James 1:12, Revelation 2:10

2. The incorruptible crown- 1Corinthians 9:25

3. The soul-winner's crown- Philippians 4:1, 1 Thessalonians 2:19

4. The crown of righteousness-2 Timothy 4:8

5. The crown of glory-1 Peter 5:4

Personal reflection: What believer's actions could be improved after considering these crowns?

SPOILER: There is a throne, a crown, a white robe, a new name and song waiting for believers! We all make up a part of the eternal worship as the bride of Christ.

NOTES OR OTHER REFERENCES

REVELATION CHAPTER 4 ANSWER KEY

1. The door

    Philadelphia, Laodicea

    Rapture of church

    The hereafter

2. The throne in heaven

    One

3. Jasper-white diamond, Sardine-red, Rainbow of emerald green

    Aaron, represented the 12 children of Israel

    An emerald rainbow

    God

4. Twenty four

    Twenty four

    Purity

    Position of being heirs to the throne and rulership with Christ

5. When God came to the Israelites at Sinai and gave Moses the ten commandments

    The fullness and completion of the Holy Spirit

    Dove, Tongues of fire

6. A sea of glass

    Seeing the lord's glory

7. Full of eyes front and back, faces of lion, man, calf, eagle, 6 wings each, never rest day or night

8. To praise the lord god almighty

    "Holy, holy, holy, is the Lord God almighty, who was and is and is to come!"

The Lord God, who is, and who was, and who is to come

9. Glory, honor, thanks

10. Fall down before Him on the throne to worship forever and ever

    Eternal

    Their crowns

11. For God's pleasure

    God's glory, honor and power

REVELATION CHAPTER 5

THE SCROLL

WEEK 4

Fill in the blanks and answer the questions below.

1. **(vs.1)** The Revelation scroll is sealed by_____ seals and written on the _____ and

   _____

   Who holds the scroll? _____

   What is unusual about this scroll?

   What do you think the contents of the scroll might be?

2. **(vs.2)** What challenge does the strong angel propose to all of creation?

   HINT: We will see this strong angel again in Revelation 10:1.

3. **(vs.3)** What strong statement is made about the scroll?

4. **(vs.4)** Why did John weep?

   HINT: When things are repeated twice be watchful of the significance.

JESUS AS THE LAMB

5. **(vs.5)** Who rescues John from his grief?

   Who did he say was worthy?

   Read Genesis 49:9, Isaiah 31:4, Hosea 11:10. All these verses speak of which animal characteristics?

Read Isaiah 11:10, Revelation 22:16. These verses speak of which family root?

In your own words give descriptors of a "lion".

6. **(vs.6)** What three things did the Lion stand in the midst of?

Complete the sentence: The Lamb looked ...

Read 1 Kings 22:11, Zechariah 1:18 for reference to 'horns of omnipotence. (Meaning the Lord is all powerful).

Read Zechariah 4:10 and 3:9 for reference to 'eyes of omniscience'. (Meaning the Lord sees and knows everything).

The eyes and horns were also considered the seven

The Holy Spirit is not only the spirit of _____ but also of _____. (See Romans 8:9)

7. **(vs.7)** From whom did the Lamb take the book?

Read Philippians 2:8-11 and tell why the Lamb was worthy to take the book?

THE SONG OF THE ELDERS & THE CHERUBIM

8. **(vs.8)** When the Lamb took the book, who fell down before him and why?

What two things did they have to hang on to as they fell down?

What was in the golden vials?

What earthly element does incense need to produce a scent?

What can you surmise from this?

9. **(vs.9)** Why was He worthy?

In Revelation 4:11 the praise was for_____and here in verse 9 it is for _____ _____Who does the song honor?

10. **(vs.10)** We are made to our God_____and_____to rule on earth.

11. **(vs.11)** Who does John see and hear join in worshipping with the elders?

How many were around the throne of God?

12. **(vs.12)** What is the proclamation of praise to the Lamb?

    What 7 words are given to Him in praise?

13. **(vs.13)** Where were the creatures that he heard speaking**?**

    Who receives their blessing, glory, honor and power?

    For how long?

14. **(vs.14)** Who gives the final word?

    What is the response of the elders?

    Who lives forever?

    What verses show which parts of the Trinity are here during this scene?

SPOILER: These things pour out God's wrath in chapters to come: 7 sealed scrolls, 7 trumpets, and 7 bowel judgements.

NOTES AND OTHER REFERENCES

REVELATION CHAPTER 5 ANSWER KEY

1. 7, Inside, Back, He who sits on the throne

   It is written inside and on outside

   Many interpretations (title deed to the earth, history of man are a few I have heard of over the years)

   Pray and find a good, trusted Biblical Commentary for interpretation

2. Who is worthy to loose the seals and open the book?

3. No man in heaven, on earth or under the earth was able to open or even look on the book

4. No man was found to open or even look on the book- verse 4 repeats verse 3

   He knew something very important was in there

5. One of the 24 elders

   The Lion of the Tribe of Judah, the Root of David

   A lion

   The Root of David

   Strong, King of Beasts, regal, stealthy, steady, majestic, etc.

6. The throne, four living creatures, 24 elders

   Slain having 7 horns and 7 eyes, Spirits of God

   God but also Christ

7. God

   Jesus was obedient to death on the cross and is ascended to heaven to the right hand of the Father

8. Four beasts and 24 elders, he took the book and He alone is worthy to open the scroll

   Harps and golden vials full of odors or incense

   The prayers of the saints

Fire

There is fire in heaven

9. He took the book and opened the seals, He was slain and has redeemed us to God by his blood out of every kindred, tongue, people and nation

    Creation, Redemption

    The Lamb

10. Kings, Priests

11. Angels

    Ten thousands of ten thousands and thousands of thousands

12. Worthy is the Lamb that was slain to receive, power, riches, wisdom, strength, honor, glory and blessing

13. In heaven, on earth, under earth, sea

    To Him who sits on the throne and the Lamb

    For ever and ever

14. Four beasts

    Fell down to worship

    God

    The Lamb- vs 5, 6, 8, 12, 13, 14, The Holy Spirit of God- 6, God- 7, 10, 13, 14

REVELATION CHAPTERS 6 AND 7

1st-6th SEALS OPEN

WEEK 5

INTRODUCTION TO THE 1ST SIX SEALS: CHAPTER 6

15. **(vs.1)** What is the scroll?
16. Who commands, "come" to the horsemen of each of the seals being opened? (Supplementary reading: Ezekiel 1:1-28)
17. Who alone is able to open the seals?
18. What did the voice of one of the four beasts sound like?

THE 4 HORSEMEN OF THE APOCALYPSE: THE FIRST 4 SEALS (REFERRED TO AS THE 70TH WEEK OF DANIEL-DANIEL 9:20-27)

19. **(vs.2) HORSEMAN #1 (SEAL 1)** (Read Matthew 24 for further description)

    Color:

    Description:

    Purpose:

    Meaning

20. **(vs.3-4) HORSEMAN #2 (SEAL 2)**

    Color:

    Description:

Purpose:

Meaning:

21. **(vs. 5-6) HORSEMAN #3 (SEAL 3)**

    Color:

    Description:

    Purpose:

    Meaning:

22. **(vs. 7-8) HORSEMAN #4 (SEAL 4)**

    Color:

    Description:

    Purpose:

    Meaning:

23. Who is still on the throne in Revelation 5:6?

    (Vs. 9-11) MARTYRS (SEAL 5)

24. **(vs.9)** For what reason had they been slain and were seen under God's throne?
25. **(vs.10)** What did they do?
26. What did they say?
27. **(vs.11)** What were they given?
28. Why?
29. Meaning?

EARTHLY AND COSMIC SIGNS BEGIN

NATURE IN TRIBULATION (SEAL 6)

30. **(vs.12)** What does John see happen?
31. What caused the great earthquake?
32. What happened to all the light on earth?
33. Can you think of another time when light was the main subject?

34. **(vs.13)** What happens to the stars?
35. What other reference to a fig tree can you find? (Read John 1:46-51)
36. What was the significance of that story?
37. **(vs.14)** What is the significance of a scroll rolling together?
38. What happens to mountains and islands?
39. **(vs.15)** Who responds in this verse?
40. What did they do?
41. **(vs.16)** Were they aware of why this was all happening?
42. **(vs.17)** What is the ominous announcement here?

CHAPTER 7

43. What shift in time occurs in the first few words of vs. 1?
44. **(vs.1)** How many angels and corners and winds?
45. Where else did we see the number 4 recently? (Read Zechariah 6:1-8 for further description)
46. What do these angels prevent?
47. **(vs.2)** What did the next angel possess?
48. **(vs.3)** What did this fifth angel tell the others?
49. **(vs.2)** How did he communicate this with them?
50. **(vs.4)** How many were sealed?
51. **(vs.5-8)** What were the names and number of the sealed people from each tribe?
52. **(vs.9)** What did John do after this shift?
53. Where was this multitude from?
54. What did they do before the throne and the Lamb?
55. **(vs.9)** What were they wearing?
56. What were they holding?
57. Why do you think this is different from the elders' response in Revelation 5:8?
58. **(vs.10)** What was the praise about to God here?
59. Who did they praise?
60. **(vs.11)** Who fell on their faces this time?
61. **(vs.12)** How many words of praise did they give to God?
62. What were these words?
63. Thinking back, what blessings have we heard given to God in the first 7 chapters of Revelation and give references?
64. **(vs.13)** What did the elder ask John?
65. Why did he ask this of John?
66. **(vs.14)** What is John's response?
67. **(vs.14)** Who is the elder talking about?
68. Why are these people wearing white robes?
69. **(vs.15)** What amazing honor do they get to perform?
70. Who will live with them?
71. **(vs.16)** What earthy discomforts will they no longer endure?

72. Why is this important symbolism (the Lamb)?
73. Who actually wipes away their tears?
74. What does this show on God's part?

SPOILER: Judgement is about to fall on mankind.

THOUGHTS ON THE BOOK OF REVELATION TO THIS POINT:

REVELATION CHAPTERS 6 AND 7 ANSWER KEY

1. The thing used to reveal the Lamb of God and His redemption of mankind
2. One of the four creatures
3. The Lamb (Jesus Christ)
4. Noisy thunder
5. White, rider had a bow, crown given him, conquering and to conquer, Antichrist on the scene (read Genesis10:8-14 –Nimrod a great hunter of man)
6. Red, power given him to take peace by sword, to kill, war erupts from peace being removed
7. Black, pair of balances in hand, measure wheat/barley and preserve oil and wine, famine/scarcity/food trouble/inflation/class separation
8. Pale green, name is Death and hades follows, power given to kill ¼ earth with sword, hunger, death and beasts, earth engulfed in war, famine and death
9. The Lamb and God
10. The Word of God and the testimony they held
11. Cried with a loud voice
12. "How long Lord until you judge and avenge our blood on them on earth?"
13. White robes
14. To rest until the fellow servants and brothers were killed as they were
15. They must wait for God's judgement which takes time, Don't take judgement into their own hands
16. The 6th seal is opened
17. The opening of the 6th seal
18. Sun became black as sack cloth and moon turns to blood
19. Genesis 1:3-5 (light), 14-19 (stars, moon), Psalms 36:9 (God's light)
20. Fell to the earth like a fig tree shaken by the wind
21. The omnipresent Lord saw Nathaniel under the fig tree, announced "behold an Israelite indeed, in whom there is no guile".
22. Nathaniel announces that Jesus is the son of God and the king of Israel
23. Revelation 5:9 speaks of Jesus being worthy to open the scroll, Luke 4:20 Jesus closed the book (scroll) and sat down
24. Moved out of their places – everything becomes on level ground
25. Kings, great men, chief captains, mighty men, bondman, freemen
26. Hid themselves in rocks and caves
27. Yes. Asked the rocks to fall on them to hide them from the face of him that sits on the throne, and from the wrath of God
28. The great day of His wrath is come and who shall be able to stand
29. After these things
30. Four
31. Four horsemen, 4 horses, 4 beasts, 4 chariots (Zechariah 6:1-8)
32. Wind from blowing on the earth, sea and trees
33. The seal of the Living God (Ezekiel 9:4 speaks of a "mark", the letter 'tau' the last letter in the Hebrew alphabet shaped like a cross)

34. Don't hurt the earth, sea or trees until we seal the servants of God
35. With a loud voice
36. 144,000 people from the tribes of the children of Israel
37. Judah, Reuben, Gad, Asher, Nephthalim, Manasses, Simeon, Levi, Issachar, Zebulon, Joseph, Benjamin, 12,000 from each (the tribe of Dan is left out perhaps because of idolatry- Genesis 49:17 but Ezekiel 48 speaks of Daniel's redemption)
38. He saw a great multitude of people that no one could count
39. All nations, kindred, people, tongues
40. They stood before the throne and the Lamb
41. White robes
42. Holding palm branches
43. Here they are standing and there they are on their faces in worship (up and down for worship as we do in our church services)
44. Salvation
45. God on the throne and the Lamb (Jesus)
46. Angels, elders and four beasts
47. Seven
48. Blessing, glory, wisdom, thanksgiving, honor, power, might
49. Revelation 4:11- glory, honor, power, creation, 5:9-you were slain and redeemed us, 5:12-power, riches, wisdom, strength, honor, glory, blessing, 5:13-blessing, honor, glory, power
50. Who are these people in white robes and where are they from?
51. It was important John knew who these people were
52. "Sir you know"
53. They came out of the Great Tribulation, washed their robes and made them white in the blood of the Lamb.
54. They are redeemed by Christ's blood (people are being saved in the tribulation)
55. They are before the throne of God and serve Him day and night in His temple
56. God will live with them
57. Hunger, thirst, sun light and heat
58. Feed them and lead them to living fountains of water
59. The slain Lamb becomes the Shepherd to care for His people
60. God
61. Great human compassion, concern, tenderness, personal contact with us, husband-like, father-like, mother-like

REVELATION CHAPTER 8

7th SEAL OPENS
THE TRUMPET JUDGEMENTS BEGIN

WEEK 6

Review of important points. Complete each sentence.

1. Chapter 5-6 revealed opening of seals 1 through
2. The scroll in Revelation 5:1 is significant of the culmination of God's
3. There was a great _____ praising God in chapter 7:9.

In this chapter you may use critical thinking, Commentary or Bible notes to determine answers.

4. **(vs.1)** What happened when Jesus opened the 7th seal on the scroll of the judgement of man? (Other scripture to read: Zephaniah 1:7)
5. Why do you think this happened?
6. **(vs.2)** How many angels were given how many trumpets?
7. What do trumpets signify? (Matthew 6:2)
8. **(vs.3)** What is the angel at the alter waiting for?
9. Why?
10. **(vs.4)** How did the prayers reach God?
11. Do you think that only happens in Revelation? (Psalms 141:2)
12. **(vs.5)** What did the angel do with the incense then?
13. **(vs.5)** What was the result?
14. What does this show us?
15. **(vs.7)** What does the first of the seven angels do?
16. **(vs.7)** What is the result?
17. In the realm of reality that we understand what might this be?
18. **(vs.8-9)** What happened when the second angel blew the trumpet?
19. **(vs.8-9)** What was the result?
20. **(vs.8-9)** What number is associated with the second trumpet?
21. What might this mean in our reality?

22. **(vs.10)** What happened when the third angel blew his trumpet?
23. **(vs.11)** What is the name of the star?
24. **(vs.11)** What happened to the water?
25. What might this mean in our reality?
26. **(vs.12)** What happened when the fourth angel blew his trumpet?
27. **(vs.12)** Result?
28. What might this mean in our reality?
29. **(vs.13)** What did John see and hear?
30. **(vs.13)** What did the angel say to the earth dwellers?
31. **(vs.13)** Why did he say this?

SPOILER: A locust invasion of Biblical proportions is about to occur!

REVELATION CHAPTER 8 ANSWER KEY

1. Six
2. God's judgment on unrepentant mankind
3. Multitude
4. Silence in heaven of ½ hour
5. Heaven is timeless and God steps into man's time for the upcoming judgements
6. Seven
7. Announcement (1 Samuel 13:3), call to worship (Isaiah 27:13), call to war (numbers 10:9-10), celebration (Numbers 29:1)
8. Incense to be given him
9. So he would offer it up with the prayers of the saints on the golden alter before the throne
10. Smoke of the incense and the prayers of the saints ascended out of the angel's hand before God
11. No, all through scripture
12. Took the empty censer and filled it with fire from the alter and threw it to the earth
13. Voices, thunders, lightning and earthquake
14. Our prayers reach God and are acted upon on earth
15. Sounds his trumpet
16. Hail and fire mixed with blood was cast to the earth destroying 1/3 trees and green grass
17. Sunspots, space junk, something we have never seen before coming from God
18. Something like a great mountain on fire was cast into the sea
19. A third of the sea became blood, third of sea creatures died, third of ships destroyed
20. One third
21. Meteorite, star, something we have not seen yet from God
22. A great star fell from heaven burning like a lamp and landed in 1/3 of the rivers and fountains of water
23. Wormwood (See Jeremiah 9:15)
24. It became bitter and undrinkable and people died
25. Water-borne diseases like dysentery and many others
26. One third sun, moon, stars darkened
27. Day and night had 1/3 less light
28. Loss of sun's heat by 1/3, growing seasons affected, oxygen affected, more storms/snow
29. An angel flying through the midst of heaven
30. "Woe, woe, woe, to the inhabitants of the earth
31. Because the trumpets of 3 more angels are yet to sound, It is about to get really intense for the people on earth

REVELATION CHAPTER 9

FIFTH AND SIXTH TRUMPETS SOUND

WEEK 7

Remember last week. We just listened to 4 of the 6 Trumpet Judgements sound. It may be helpful to go back to last week to remember those first 4 to keep your momentum of thought moving forward. This week the 5th and 6th Trumpet Judgements will sound.

1. **(vs.1)** What happened when the 5th angel sounded the trumpet?
2. **(vs.1)** What was he given?
3. What might this be saying about "the star"?
4. **(vs.2-3)** What happened when this "star" unlocked the bottomless pit?
5. **(vs.2)** Was it actually a furnace?
6. **(vs.2)** What happened to the sun and the air?
7. **(vs.3)** What came out of the smoke?
8. What power is given to earthly locusts and what do they normally eat?
9. **(vs.4)** What were the locusts not to hurt?
10. **(vs.4)** What were they commanded to hurt?
11. **(vs.5)** Are they to kill these men?
12. **(vs.5)** What are they allowed to do?
13. **(vs.5)** How long?
14. **(vs.5)** What is their torment of man like?
15. **(vs.6)** Complete the sentence: At that time men will seek death but will not

LOCUST DESCRIPTION

16. Why might we be given this precise description of the locusts?

   Finish each description below:

17. **(vs.7)** Shaped like:
18. **(vs.7)** On their heads:

19. **(vs.7)** Their faces looked like:
20. **(vs.8)** Their hair looked like:
21. **(vs.8)** Their teeth were like:
22. **(vs.9)** They wore:
23. **(vs.9)** Their wings sounded like:
24. **(vs.10)** Their tales were like:
25. **(vs.10)** What could they do with their tails:
26. **(vs.10)** Their power was to:
27. What does vs. 11 say about their king"?
28. **(vs.11)** What is the king's description?
29. In Hebrew what is the name **(vs.11)**_____ in Greek **(vs.11)**
30. What does Proverbs 30:27 say about actual earthy locusts and what can we assume about the locusts in this chapter? (Are they talking about the same type of locusts?)

THE LOCUSTS PURPOSE/COMMANDMENT ANNOUNCEMENT

31. **(vs.12)** The first_____is past!
32. **(vs.12)** How many more woes are coming?

6TH TRUMPET/WOE #2

33. **(vs.13-14)** When the 6th angel blew the 6th trumpet where did a voice come from?
34. Thinking back to Revelation 8:3, what occurred at the golden alter?

PRAYERS ARE VERY IMPORTANT IN TIMES OF TROUBLE!!

35. Exodus 30:1-10 speaks of another alter. Where was this alter and what did Aaron do there?
36. Were prayers offered on this alter?
37. What was offered?
38. Read Exodus 29:44-46. How do these verses parallel heaven?
39. **(vs.14)** What did the voice in tell the 6th angel to do?
40. **(vs.15)** Were these angels/creatures released at a random time?
41. Why are they bound in the Euphrates River? (See Genesis 15:18 regarding the boundaries of the Israeli promised land.)

INTERESTING FACTS ABOUT THE EUPHRATES RIVER IN SCRIPTURE AND EXAMPLES OF EVIL IN THE LAND

Genesis 2:10-14   First mention of the Euphrates as a landmark

Genesis 4   First murder- Cain kills Abel/blood spilt on the ground

Genesis 10:8-10   First hunter of man

Genesis 11:1-9   First corporate revolt against God, building a tower to heaven

Genesis 14:1   First war pact of kings, destroy many cities in the land

42. **(vs.16)** How may horsemen are in this army?
43. How many men will they kill?
44. Who is in control of the Tribulation? (See Revelation 19:6)
45. Whose will is it that allows this killing of the 1/3 of men? (See Revelation 22:6)

THE 200 MILLION MAN ARMY

46. **(vs.17)** What were the army men wearing?
47. **(vs.17)** What colors were in the breastplate?
48. Where is the armour of God found in the Bible?
49. According to Ephesians 6:14 and 1 Thessalonians 5:8, what does our breastplate signify?
50. What does the evil army breastplate signify?

REMEMBER THAT SATAN ALWAYS TRIES TO IMITATE GOD IN PURPOSE BUT WITH HIS OWN MOTIVES.

51. **(vs.17)** What came out of their horse heads (that looked like lions heads)?
52. **(vs.18-19)** What 3 things killed 1/3 of men?
53. **(vs.19)** Where is their power from and to what does John relate their power?
54. **(vs.20)** What "works of their hands" did the remaining 2/3 of mankind refuse to repent of?
55. Read Deuteronomy 4:28-31. What is this speaking of?
56. Read 1 Corinthians 10:20. To what are they sacrificing?
57. Could this be a reference to what men in Revelation are sacrificing to?
58. **(vs.21)** What is on the list of the non-repentant sins?

Other BIBLICAL examples of supernatural armies

2 Kings 2:11   Elijah's translation

2 Kings 6:14-17   Elisha asks for Syrian soldiers blindness

Revelation 19:14 Christ's second coming!

SPOILER: Two mysterious witnesses are coming! Who might they be?

REVELATION CHAPTER 9 ANSWER KEY

1. A star fell from heaven to the earth
2. The key to the bottomless pit
3. Is not a star but an actual being (Read Revelation 20:1-3)
4. Smoke came out like a furnace
5. Verse 2 states it is "like the smoke of a great furnace"
6. They were darkened by the smoke of the pit
7. Locusts
8. To sting with their tails, they normally eat green vegetation
9. The Grass of the earth or any green tree
10. Only those people without the seal of God on their foreheads
11. No
12. To torment these people for five months
13. Five months
14. Like the sting of a scorpion when it stings a man
15. Seek death and death will run from them
16. It is the Lord's nature to be kind and protective (Read Psalms 117:1-2)
17. Like horses prepared to go into battle
18. Crowns like gold
19. Men's faces
20. Women's hair
21. Lions
22. Breastplates of iron
23. Chariots with many horses running into battle
24. Scorpion's tails
25. Sting
26. Hurt people for five months
27. He was a king over them
28. Angel of the bottomless pit
29. Abaddon
30. Apollyon
31. Woe
32. Two
33. The four horns of the golden altar which is before God
34. The angel offered the prayers of all the saints there
35. In the tabernacle of God, Aaron made a blood atonement for the people on the horns of the alter once per year
36. No. Blood offering was performed in the tabernacle of God in the desert
37. Only blood as a sin offering
38. The heavenly alter has a different meaning, On earth the alter was for salvation. In heaven the alter is for the redeemed.
39. Loose the four angels bound in the great Euphrates river

40. They are prepared for an hour, a day, a month and a year; Nothing is random with God's time schedule, This is a day on a calendar and an hour on that day

41. The Euphrates is the border of the Promised Land given by God to the Israelites; Much evil is done in the land of the Garden of Eden and beyond

42. 200,000,000 (two hundred million) horsemen

43. One third of the population

44. The Lord God

45. God's will

46. Breast plates

47. Fiery red, hyacinth blue, sulfur yellow

48. Ephesians 6:10-18, I Thessalonians 5:8

49. The righteousness of Christ as well as faith and love

50. Death and destruction

51. Fire and smoke and brimstone

52. Fire and smoke and brimstone killed one third of mankind

53. Their mouths and their tails, tails like serpents and heads which hurt people

54. Worshipping the works of their hands; Devils and idols of gold, silver, brass, stone and wood which can't see, hear or walk

55. The longsuffering mercy of God

56. Devils, not to God

57. Yes, devils and evil

58. Murder, sorceries, fornication and theft

REVELATION CHAPTERS 10 AND 11

JOHN AND THE LITTLE BOOK
TWO WITNESSES ARRIVE

WEEK 8

Now we have a short break in the story. Chapter 9 ended with the blowing of the 6th trumpet to begin the end of all things. These 2 chapters are exciting with extensive information so buckle up and get ready to fly!

ANOTHER ANGEL

1. (vs.1) What is this angel from heaven wearing on his head? On his face? On his feet?
2. Who does Revelation 1:15-16 refer to?
3. Is Jesus ever referred to as just an "angel"?
4. Who is referred to in Daniel 12:1 & 12:6-7?
5. (vs.2) What does the angel hold in his right hand?
6. Does this "little book" fit the description of the book in Revelation 5:1?
7. (vs.2) Where is his right foot? Left foot?
8. What might this signify?
9. (vs.3) What did his loud voice resemble and what happened when he cried out?
10. Read Psalms 29 and Job 37: 4-5. Whose voice thunders here?
11. (vs.4) What happened when John began to write what the 7 thunders said?
12. What does this show us about Revelation?
13. (vs.5-6) What does the angel with feet on land and seas do here?
14. What is the definition of "oath"? (May use any source.)
15. (vs.6) Which attribute of God is praised?
16. (vs.6) What creations is God praised for?
17. (vs.6) What ominous statement is at the end of the oath?
18. (vs.7) Which upcoming angel is referred to here?
19. (vs.7) What happens when he blows his trumpet?
20. (vs.7) Who did he declare this to?

21. Read Amos 3:6-8. Why is this significant?
22. **(vs.8)** What does the voice from heaven tell John to do?
23. **(vs.9)** What instruction did the angel give to John?
24. **(vs.9)** What would be the physical outcome of this instruction?
25. **(vs.10)** Did John experience what the angel told him?
26. What do you think this is significant of?
27. **(vs.11)** What does the angel tell John he must do?
28. To whom must he do this?
29. Who do you think this refers to?

CHAPTER 11- THE TWO WITNESSES COME ON THE SCENE

30. **(vs.1)** What was given to John? Why?
31. Other examples of "measuring". Ezekiel 40, Habakkuk 3:6, Zechariah 2, Revelation 21.

    Notes:

32. What does the term "measuring" often refer to?
33. **(vs.1-2)** In the big scheme of Revelation, what might "temple of God" mean?
34. Briefly scan Ezekiel 40-43. What is happening there?
35. How does Luke 21:24 relate to Revelation 1-2?
36. **(vs2)** How long do the Gentiles tread on the Holy City?
37. **(vs.3)** How long will the 2 witnesses prophecy?
38. **(vs.3)** What will the 2 witnesses be wearing?
39. What is sackcloth? And what is it for? (Use any source.)
40. **(vs.4)** What is the significance of the two olive trees? (See Zechariah 4) and the two candlesticks?
41. **(vs.4)** Who do they stand before?
42. Any ideas of who the 2 witnesses in the Old Testament might be?
43. Read the following and comment on who the two witnesses might be.

    Exodus 7:20

    Exodus 8:1-12:29

    1 Kings 17:1

    1 Kings 18:41-45

    2 Kings 1:10-14

44. **(vs.5-6)** What in these verses might cause us to draw conclusions on who the 2 witnesses might be?
45. **(vs.7)** When does this progression occur?

46. Why is this an important statement?

47. **(vs.7)** Who makes war against the 2 witnesses?

48. Where did we see a reference to "The Bottomless Pit" before?

49. **(vs7)** What three things does God allow to happen to the witnesses?

50. **(vs.8)** Where do their dead bodies lie?

51. **(vs.8)** What does the verse tell us is important about "Sodom and Egypt"?

52. What cities do these references refer to? Isaiah 1:9, Genesis 13:12, 18:20-21?

53. **(vs.9)** Who will see their dead bodies?

54. **(vs.9)** How long will they see their bodies?

55. **(vs.9)** Will they receive the dignity of a burial?

56. What does this say about those around them?

57. **(vs.10)** What is the response of those who dwell on the earth?

58. **(vs.10)** What is their perception of the 2 witnesses?

59. **(vs.11)** What happens to the 2 witnesses after 3 ½ days?

60. **(vs.11)** Who gave them life according to verse?

61. **(vs.11)** What is the response of the world?

62. **(vs.12)** What caused them to depart?

63. **(vs.12)** Who watched them depart in a cloud?

64. Read 2 Kings 2:11 and tell who else was supernaturally taken to heaven?

65. **(vs.13)** What else happens within 60 minutes of them being taken?

66. **(vs.13)** How much of the city was destroyed and how many men were killed?

67. **(vs.13)** What was the remnant's response?

68. Remember Revelation 9:21. What did they not do?

69. **(vs.14)** What is the ominous statement here?

70. **(vs.14)** This shows us what about the previous section?

71. **(vs.14)** What does this show about the coming section?

72. **(vs.15)** When the 7th trumpet sounds what 2 statements are made from heaven?

73. This signifies:

74. **(vs.16)** What did the 24 elders do at this declaration?

75. Do you remember where in Revelation we saw this before?

76. **(vs.17)** What do they give to the Lord God Almighty?

77. **(vs.17)** Why?

78. **(vs.18)** How did the nations respond?

79. **(vs.18)** What time has come?

80. **(vs.18)** What 2 different types of judgement are delineated among the dead?

81. **(vs.19)** When the scene switches to the temple what is seen there?

82. **(vs.19)** What is the response of all of creation?

SPOILER: What do a woman and her child, a dragon, the moon and sun have in common? War!

REVELATION CHAPTERS 10 AND 11 ANSWER KEY

1. Crown, rainbow, sun
2. Jesus
3. No, Hebrews 2:16
4. Michael, "the great Prince"
5. A little open book
6. No, seems to be a different book
7. Sea, Earth
8. Authority over all creation, omnipresent God
9. Lion's roar or cry, Seven thunders sounded noise
10. The Lord
11. He was told to seal up those things which the seven thunders uttered, see Daniel 8:26, 12:9
12. It is a mystery and not all God's mysteries are meant to be revealed until it is God's time
13. He lifted up his hand to heaven
14. "A formal declaration or pledge calling on God as a witness" –Webster's Dictionary
15. God's eternal state and his creator status
16. Heaven and contents, Earth and contents, Sea and contents
17. There should be no more time! Time is up as we know it
18. Seventh angel
19. The mystery of God is finished
20. His servants, the prophets
21. It proofs the Old Testament with the New Testament, God eventually reveals all his mysteries to us
22. Go to the angel with his foot on the land and sea and take the open little book
23. Take it and eat the book
24. It will taste like honey but will make his stomach bitter
25. Yes
26. Reading the Word of God is sweet to our soul but judgements of God are like bitterness
27. Prophesy again
28. Many peoples, nations, tongues and kings
29. All people down through history from the point of his vision, You and me!
30. A reed to be used like a measuring rod or stick, to measure the temple and alter of God and worshippers
31. Extra reading about measuring
32. Measuring out Judgements of God
33. Physical temple during time of Tribulation made by Israel, worshippers, Millennial Temple (Ezekiel 40-48 for extra reading)
34. Israel is rebuilding a Temple, renewing relationship with God
35. The Gentile domination of Jerusalem began with Nebuchadnezzar in 587 B.C. through A.D. 70 through today and until the time of the Tribulation
36. Forty two months
37. 1,260 days which is 3 ½ years

38. Sackcloth
39. Coarsely woven fabric usually made from goat hair used for mourning, 2 Samuel 3:31, Jonah 3:5
40. Oil in the lamps of the witnesses of God
41. The God of the earth
42. May use creative thinking
43. Moses (and Aaron), Moses, Elijah, Elijah, Elijah
44. Because of the correlation of the miraculous signs performed through these two and the two witness of God
45. When their testimony is done, 1,260 days
46. It is the completion of God's final witness and grace to call evil man
47. The beast from the bottomless pit
48. Revelation 9:1, Satan
49. Make war with them, Overcome them, Kill them
50. In the streets of Sodom and Egypt
51. The Lord Jesus was crucified there
52. Jerusalem compared to Sodom and Egypt
53. All people, kindred, tongues, nations
54. 3 ½ days
55. No, they lay in the streets unburied
56. Calloused, hateful, resentful, fearful
57. They make merry and rejoice sending gifts to each other because the 2 tormenting prophets are dead
58. Torment people
59. The Spirit of life from God enters them and they stand on their feet
60. The Spirit of God
61. Great fear falls on them
62. A great voice from heaven calls them to "Come up here"
63. Their enemies
64. Elijah
65. A great earthquake occurred
66. A 10th of the city was destroyed and 7,000 men killed
67. They were fearful and gave glory to God
68. They did not Repent, No mention of repentance
69. The 2nd Woe is past, the 3rd woe comes quickly
70. It was very important
71. Something very important is about to occur
72. "The kingdoms of this world are become the kingdoms of our Lord and of his Christ"; "He shall reign forever and ever"
73. God is in control and has all power over heaven and earth, He is usurping supreme rulership
74. Fell on their faces and worshipped God
75. Revelation 4:10, 5:8
76. Thanks to the Lord God Almighty
77. He is, was and is to come and has taken to himself his great power and will reign

78. The nations were angry
79. Time for the judgement of the dead, servants and prophets
80. Rewards to the servants and prophets and saints that fear his name, destruction to those who destroy the earth
81. The Ark of the Testament (Covenant) of God
82. There came lightning, voices, thunder, earth quake and hail

REVELATION CHAPTER 12

WARS ON EARTH AND IN HEAVEN
THE WOMAN AND THE DRAGON

WEEK 9

Remember as we move forward that the "End of Time" has been announced. Why then do we continue on with a war this week? Revelation is not all in succession. The time frames may overlap as the chapters progress. Also symbolism often represents reality in God's terms. Read on to understand.

1. **(vs.1)** What great sign appeared in heaven?
2. **(vs.1)** What was the woman clothed with? What was on her feet and her head?
3. Read Genesis 37:9-11 and tell whose dream is similar to this part of Revelation 12.
4. Read Galatians 4:26. Who does this refer to as "the mother of us all"?

   For your own reading: Other references Isaiah 54:1-8, Jeremiah 3:20, Ezekiel 16:8-16, Hosea 2:19-20

5. **(vs.2)** What did the woman do?
6. **(vs.2)** What 2 descriptors were said about the birth?
7. Read Isaiah 13:6-13. What "day" is mentioned here and who is having birth pangs in verses 7-8?
8. **(vs.3)** What sign then appeared in the heavens?

   Search to try to find a meaning in any scripture texts for items in this scripture verse. (May use Commentary or study aids.)

Color of the dragon?   Meaning: (Revelation 9:17)
Number of heads?   Meaning: (Revelation 2:4)
Number of horns?   Meaning: (Daniel 7:7, 21)
Number of crowns?   Meaning: (Revelation 9:7)

9. **(vs.4)** What did the dragon's tail do?
10. **(vs.4)** What is the dragon waiting for?
11. What is the dragon trying to do to the 'man child' through Herod in Matthew 2:16-18?
12. **(vs.5)** What is the man child prophesied to do?
13. **(vs.5)** Where is the child taken to?
14. **(vs.6)** Where does the woman flee to and why?
15. **(vs.6)** How long will she be there?
16. What does Matthew 24:15-23 say about the Judean people?

WAR IN THE HEAVENS

17. **(vs.7)** Where does this battle take place?
18. **(vs.7)** Who are the characters fighting this battle?
19. **(vs.8)** What domain is the devil trying to conquer?
20. **(vs.9)** What happened to the dragon and his angels?
21. **(vs.9)** What is the consequence of this?
22. What does Jude 9 say is Michael's title?
23. What valuable lesson do we learn from Michael's response to Satan in Jude?
24. **(vs.9)** What 4 names are used?
25. **(vs.9)** What is Satan's purpose?

HEAVENLY VICTORY!

26. **(vs.10)** What did John hear from heaven?
27. **(vs.10)** What 4 thing have come after the battle?

    1.
    2.
    3.
    4.

28. **(vs.10)** Why were these things possible?
29. **(vs.10)** What do we learn about Satan in that can help us in our current lives?
30. **(vs.11)** What post-war benefits do we as believer's have?
31. **(vs.11)** Do we triumph in our own strength?
32. **(vs.11)** Do we have to fight to get this benefit?
33. **(vs.11)** What 3 things allow us to be victorious?

    1.
    2.
    3.

34. (**vs.12**) Who is rejoicing?
35. (**vs.12**) What woe is pronounced to the earth and sea dwellers?
36. (**vs.12**) What does the devil know that makes him furious?

THE DRAGON PURSUES THE WOMAN AND HER OFFSPRING

37. (**vs.13**) Why does the dragon pursue the woman and her son?
38. (**vs.14**) What allows the women to fly to the wilderness?
39. Read Exodus 19:4, Deuteronomy 32:10-12. What do these two verses allude to?
40. (**vs.14**) How long is the woman hidden from the face of the serpent?
41. (**vs.15**) What does the serpent try to do to the woman?
42. (**vs.16**) How does the earth help her out?
43. Read Hosea 5:10, Deuteronomy 27:17, Psalm 32:6, Psalm 93:2-4.

    What do these verses imply about boundaries? About water?

44. (**vs.17**) What is the dragon's response to woman?
45. (**vs.17**) Who does the dragon go to make war with?
46. (**vs.17**) What are the remnant's characteristics?

SPOILER: The Antichrist shows off his new Lieutenant, the False Prophet who begins a process of marking people. (P.S. If you are left behind, here are 2 tips: 1. Admit you are a sinner in need of a savior and accept Christ as your King as soon as possible. 2. Do not take the mark of the beast! There is no going back to Christ once you have made allegiance to the Antichrist.

REVELATION CHAPTER 12 ANSWER KEY

1. A woman clothed in the sun
2. Clothed with the sun, Moon under her feet, Crown of 12 stars on her head
3. Joseph
4. Jerusalem, Israel
5. Being with child she cried
6. Travailed, Pain
7. Day of the Lord, all people on the earth will understand birth pangs
8. Another sign, a great red dragon

    Color of the dragon: Red, Fiery red breastplate

    Seven heads, Seven churches

    Ten horns, Antichrist, 10 nations

    Seven crowns, Crown of false rulership

9. Pulled 1/3 part of the stars to the earth
10. 10.To eat the woman's child
11. Kill Jesus, the man child
12. To rule the nations with a rod of iron
13. Taken up to God and his throne
14. Flees to the wilderness prepared by God, Someone will feed them there
15. 1,260 days, the last 3 ½ years of the tribulation
16. They should flee to the mountains, take nothing from home, if in a field run, pregnant should pray they leave in summer and not on Sabbath, don't believe in Christ-imitators
17. Heavens
18. Michael and his angels, the dragon and his angels
19. Heaven
20. They lost the battle
21. They lost their place in heaven
22. Archangel
23. We need only let the Lord rebuke Satan
24. Great dragon, Old serpent, Devil, Satan
25. To deceive the whole world
26. A loud voice
27. Salvation, Strength, Kingdom of our God, Power of His Christ (Authority)
28. The accuser of the brothers has been cast down
29. God is in control, Satan only has power allowed by God
30. The ability to overcome the devil
31. No
32. No

33. Blood of the Lamb, Word of their testimony, Love not life unto death
34. Heaven dwellers
35. The Devil has come down to them
36. He knows he only has a short time left
37. He saw he was cast to the earth
38. Wings of a great eagle
39. Deliverance from God
40. 3 ½ years
41. Makes a flood of water to go after the woman
42. Opens to swallow the water
43. It is illegal to move God's boundaries between God and man which are secure, the floods may rise up but God is mightier
44. The dragon is angry
45. The remnant of her seed
46. They keep the commandments of God and have the testimony of Jesus Christ

REVELATION CHAPTER 13

THE BEAST AND HIS FALSE PROPHET

WEEK 10

This week we have a new character come on the scene. He is 3rd person of the unholy trinity of Satan, the Antichrist and now the Antichrist's helper, false prophet, Lieutenant. Beware the "Mark of the Beast"!

1. From Revelation 12: Who is the dragon? Who is the woman? To whom did the woman give birth?
    Revelation 13:
2. **(vs.1)** The "I" refers to whom?
3. **(vs.1)** Where was John standing and what did he see?
4. **(vs.1)** Describe the beast (the Antichrist).
5. Who in chapter 12 has a similar description?
6. What is the difference in the number of crowns of the dragon and the beast (Antichrist)?
7. Crowns even today represent what?
8. What does Daniel 7:24 say about the Horns?
9. What does this Daniel passage say the diverse king shall subdue?
10. Consider Daniel chapters 2 and 7 which describe the past Roman empires. When the 4th kingdom arises in Daniel 2:44 who is in power?
11. **(vs.1)** Back in Revelation 13, what is written on "his heads"?
12. From any source, what is the definition of blasphemy?
13. **(vs.2)** Describe the beast (Antichrist).
14. **(vs.2)** From Revelation 12:9, who is the dragon?
15. **(vs.2)** What 3 things did the dragon give the beast?
16. What did Jesus refuse in Matthew 4:8-10 that the beast (Antichrist) now accepts?
17. Read 1 John 2:18, 22 and 4:3, 2 John 7. Who do these verses refer to?
18. From any source, what is the definition of "antichrist"?
19. Give the title or description of the Antichrist in the references listed:

    Daniel 7:7-8

    Daniel 8:23

Matthew 24:24

2 Thessalonians 2:3

20. In John 17:12, who else is called "Son of perdition"?
21. What do he and the beast have in common?
22. **(vs.3)** What type of wound does John see on the beast's head and what does the world do when they see this?
23. In John 20 who was resurrected from the dead?
24. Does it appear that the beast (Antichrist) is trying to imitate Jesus' resurrection from the dead?
25. **(vs.4)** What is the order of worship here?
26. **(vs.4)** What do the worshippers proclaim about the beast?
27. **(vs.5)** What permission was given to the beast to speak and how long did he say it?
28. **(vs.6)** Which 3 blasphemies does the Antichrist speak out?
29. **(vs.7)** What 2 purposes are given the beast here?
30. **(vs.8)** What is the "earth dwellers" response?
31. **(vs.8)** What is the critical description of these people?
32. **(vs.8)** From when was the Lamb slain?
33. In Revelation 17:8, what else is known from the foundation of the earth?
34. **(vs.9)** What declaration is said here?
35. What does Proverbs 18:15 say about "the ear"?
36. **(vs.10)** What 2 persecution modes are listed and what happens to those people who do this?
37. **(vs.10)** What 2 Christian attributes are we to use during persecution and what assurance as a believer does this verse give?

THE FALSE PROPHET OF THE ANTICHRIST ARRIVES!

38. **(vs.11)** Where does the next beast (False Prophet) come from and what is his description?
39. In Revelation 5:6 who is the Lamb?
40. **(vs.12)** The other beast (False Prophet) exercises all the power of the first beast (Antichrist). What is this power? See Revelation 13:1-8.
41. **(vs.12)** Whom does he cause to worship the first beast and why?
42. Who is the first beast?
    The second beast?

THE POWER OF THE SECOND BEAST (FALSE PROPHET)

43. **(vs.13)** What great miracle does he perform?
44. Who else sent fire from heaven in 2 Kings 1:10-15?
45. **(vs.14)** Who is this second beast attempting to deceive?
46. **(vs.14)** In front of whom did the 2nd beast have power to do miracles?
47. What commandment is given to the people?

48. How does verse 14 say the death of the beast (Antichrist) occurred in vs 12?
49. **(vs.15)** After the beast was given life, what 2 powers are given to "the image of the beast"?
50. **(vs.16)** Who does the Antichrist's counterpart cause to receive a mark?
51. **(vs.16)** Where is the mark to be placed and what is the purpose of the mark?
52. **(vs.17)** What are the 3 ways you can buy or sell?
53. **(vs.18)** What is wisdom here and what is the number that tells who the Antichrist is?
54. What does it seem like the relationship is between the first beast and the second beast?

SPOILER: There is an upcoming new song sung before the throne! Get ready to listen and sing.

Some current events may actually fit in this chapter. Consider meanings in light of these events in relationship to: receiving a mark, a man who will rule the world and the people. Every generation since Jesus' resurrection thought they were the generation to see the Lord. Watch and pray.

REVELATION CHAPTER 13 ANSWER KEY

1. Dragon=Satan, Woman=Israel, Woman gave birth to man child/Messiah/Jesus

2. John
3. Sand of the sea, beast coming out of the sea
4. 7 heads with blasphemy written on them, 10 horns, 10 crowns
5. The Red Dragon
6. Dragon has 7 and Beast has 10
7. Royalty, Rulership, Nations, National Power
8. Ten horns are 10 kings
9. Three kings will be subdues
10. The God of Heaven
11. Blasphemy
12. Insulting or contempt for God, claiming attributes of deity
13. Like a leopard with feet of a bear and mouth of a lion
14. Satan
15. Power, his seat (or position), his authority
16. Earthly Kingdoms and worship of Satan
17. Worldly antichrist-types
18. Deniers of Christ, antagonist who fills the world with wickedness
19. Forth Beast, Little Horn, King of fierce countenance, False Christ, false prophet, Man of sin, Son of perdition
20. Judas
21. Both antichrists, betrayers and deniers of God
22. One of his heads was wounded to death and healed, people were astonished, surprised, amazed, had admiration
23. Jesus
24. Yes
25. They worshipped Satan who gave power to the beast and then they worship the second beast
26. Who is like the beast and who can make war with him
27. He is given a mouth to speak great things to the people including blasphemy for 42 months
28. He blasphemes against God's name, His tabernacle and the beings in heaven
29. He is given power to make war with the saints and overcome them
30. The worship Satan or the other beast
31. Those whose names are not written in the Lamb's Book of Life
32. From the foundation of the world
33. Whose names were not written in the Book of Life from the foundation of the world
34. If anyone has an ear let him hear
35. The ear of the wise seeks knowledge
36. Being taken to prison (captivity) or killed with the sword, whatever they do to persecute others will happen to them
37. Patience and Faith, When we are persecuted God is working to judge the persecutors

38. Comes out of the earth, Has 2 horns like a lamb and speaks like a Dragon (Satan)
39. Jesus
40. Power, Authority, Position, Was worshipped
41. The whole earth, The deadly wound was healed
42. The Antichrist, The Antichrist's lieutenant or false prophet (Third member of the Satanic Trinity-Satan, Antichrist and False Prophet)
43. Fire from heaven to earth in sight of man
44. God
45. People who live on earth
46. The beast or Antichrist
47. Make an image of the beast (Antichrist)
48. By a sword
49. He will give life to the image of the beast, He will make it speak
50. All people, small and great, rich and poor, free and bond
51. On (or in as the KJV says) the right hand or forehead, So you can buy or sell
52. To have the Mark or the name of the Antichrist or the Number of his name
53. To have understanding to count the number of the beast, It is the number of a man, Number 666
54. Beast is the Antichrist, the second beast comes out of humanity (vs.11) and is the enforcer of the worship of the Antichrist and his image

REVELATION CHAPTER 14

THE 144,000, BEAST WORSHIP
AND EARTH HARVEST

WEEK 11

1. **(vs.1)** Who is standing on Mount Zion?
2. In contrast to the mark in Revelation 13:16-17, whose mark is on the 144,000 foreheads?
3. **(vs.2)** What 3 sounds does John hear as a "voice"?
4. Where have we seen these things before?
5. **(vs.3)** Who sang the new song?
6. **(vs.3)** Who did they sing in front of?
7. **(vs.3)** Why was the 'New Song' unique?
8. **(vs.4-5)** Give the 4 characteristics of the 144,000.

    1.
    2.
    3.
    4.

9. **(vs.5)** How do they stand before the throne of God?
10. **(vs.6)** What did the next flying angel have?
11. **(vs.7)** What 3 commands did the angel give to the people?

    1.
    2.
    3.

12. **(vs.7)** Why were they to do this?
13. **(vs.8)** What did the next angel say?
14. **(vs.8)** What is the description of Babylon?
15. **(vs.8)** Why did Babylon fall?
16. What can you find out about Babylon in 2 Kings 24 and 25?

17. **(vs.9-10)** What was the 3rd angel's warning?
18. What other references are there for 'the wine' and 'the cup' throughout scripture?
19. **(vs. 10)** How will those who receive 'the mark' be tormented?
20. **(vs.10)** Who are they in the presence of at this time?
21. **(vs.11)** What 2 details are given of those who worship the beast and his image and receive his mark?
22. **(vs.12)** What is this verse saying?
23. **(vs.13)** What did the voice tell John to do?
24. **(vs.13)** What is the blessing here?
25. **(vs.13)** What does the Spirit say is part of this blessing?
26. **(vs.13)** What does this mean; "their works follow them"?
27. **(vs.14)** What does John see on the cloud?
28. **(vs.14)** Who is the Son of man?
29. **(vs.14)** What is on his head? Meaning?
30. **(vs.14)** What is in his hand? Meaning?
31. **(vs.15)** What did the angel who came out of the temple tell the one on the cloud?

THE HARVEST IS RIPE

32. **(vs.15)** What does it mean the harvest of the earth is ripe?
33. **(vs.16)** How much effort did it take for him to reap?
34. **(vs.17)** Why do you think a second angel came out?
35. **(vs.18)** Where did the angel come from and what power does he have?
36. **(vs.18)** Who is the angel reaping now?
37. What can you find in scripture relating to grapes?
38. What is different in vs. 19 from the reaping that occurred in vs. 16?
39. **(vs.20)** Where was the winepress?
40. **(vs.20)** What came out of the winepress? How deep?

SPOILER: Seven bowls are filled with 7 plagues and will be poured out on earth.

What new facts did you learn about in this section in Revelation?

REVELATION CHAPTER 14 ANSWER KEY

1. A Lamb and the 144,000 people
2. The Lamb's Father, God
3. Many waters (Revelation 1:15), Great Thunder (Revelation 4:5, 6:1), Harpists (Revelation 5:8)
4. Revelation 1:15-God,

    Revelation 4:5-Thunder, lightning, voices from the throne,

    Revelation 6:1-A voice like thunder,

    Revelation 5:8- The four beasts and the 24 elders all had harps

5. The 144,000 with harps playing
6. The throne, the 4 beasts and the elders
7. No one could learn it except the 144,000
8. Not defiled with women (virgins),

    They follow the Lamb wherever he goes,

    Redeemed from among men as first fruits to God and the Lamb,

    There is no guile in their mouth

9. They stand faultless before the throne
10. The everlasting Gospel to preach to them on the earth (God's last call of grace to mankind on earth)
11. Fear God

    Give glory to him

    Worship him that made heaven and earth and sea and the fountains of water

12. The hour of his judgment has come, The last call for repentance
13. "Babylon is fallen, is fallen"
14. That great city
15. She made all nations drink the wine of the wrath of her fornication
16. Nebuchadnezzar was king, came against Israel twice (2 Kings 24:10, 25:2), Stole the treasures of the Temple under Solomon's rule
17. If you worship the beast (Antichrist) and his image and receive the Mark of the Beast on your hand or forehead, you will drink the wine of the wrath of God
18. 18.Judgement- Jeremiah 25:15, Psalm 75:8, Exposure of the truth- Proverbs 23:31, Cup of Salvation- Psalm 116:13, New Testament Cup- I Corinthians 11:25-29, Jesus' Cup- Matthew 26:39

19. With fire and brimstone

20. In the presence of the holy angels and the Lamb

21. The smoke of their torment goes up forever and ever, They have no rest neither day nor night

22. Know that our rest as believers in Christ is coming, be courageous and patient in keeping the commandments of God

23. Write

24. If you die in the Lord from this time forward it is a blessing

25. Rest from their labors

26. Their works will follow them into the judgement

27. One like the Son of man

28. Jesus (Revelation 1:13, 1 John 3:8)

29. A Golden Crown meaning Dominion or Rulership

30. A sharp sickle meaning time to Reap

31. "Thrust in your sickle and reap; for the time is come for you to reap; for the harvest of the earth is ripe."

32. All eternal choices have been made! There is no more time for any planting, watering or growth

33. No effort, was instantaneous

34. He came out of the temple so perhaps his reaping was in response to the prayers of the saints (Revelation 5:8)

35. He came from the alter and had power over fire

36. The rest of humanity will be reaped and brought to the Valley of Jehoshaphat (or the valley of decision) Read Joel chapter 3.

37. Grapes of gall-Deuteronomy 32:32, Wild grapes-Isaiah 5:4, Sour grapes-Ezekiel 18:2, Abundance of wine-Genesis 49:11, Grapes as fruit-Luke 6:44, Matthew 7:16

38. In vs.16 the Earths' harvest is ripe and reaped. In verse 19 the harvest is cast into the winepress. In the Ryrie Study Bible, Walvoord is reported as using the words, "Great human carnage" about this time.

39. Outside the city (Hebrews 13:12-Jesus suffered outside the city)

40. Blood came out of the winepress in a stream 200 miles long and 4 ½ feet deep (a reference to Armageddon)

REVELATION CHAPTERS 15 AND 16

SEVEN ANGELS WITH SEVEN BOWL JUDGMENTS

WEEK 12

CH 15- JUST PRIOR TO THE FINAL BOWL JUDGEMENTS

1. **(vs.1)** What wonder does John see in heaven?
2. **(vs.1)** What is significant about the last 7 plagues?
3. **(vs.2)** What did the sea look like?
4. What do the following verses say about glass?

   1 Corinthians 13:12-

   2 Corinthians 3:18-

   James 1:23-

5. **(vs.2)** What are the 4 qualifiers of them who stand on the sea of glass?

   1.
   2.
   3.
   4.

6. **(vs.2)** What are these people holding?
7. **(vs.3)** What are they singing?
8. Read Exodus 15:1-21. What is the subject of Moses' song?
9. **(vs.4)** What praises do the people give God?
10. **(vs.4)** What is the reason they are praising?
11. **(vs.5)** What was opened?
12. What does this make you think we will be doing in heaven?
13. **(vs.6)** How many angels came out?

14. **(vs.6)** How many plagues?
15. **(vs.6)** What were they wearing?
16. Thinking back to Revelation 1:13, the girdle is clothing worn by whom in the temple?
17. **(vs.7)** Who is the subject here?
18. Where in our study of Revelation did we see this before?
19. **(vs.7)** Who are the 4 beasts?
20. **(vs.7)** What are the angels given?
21. **(vs.8)** With what was the temple filled?
22. **(vs. 8)** When were men allowed to go back into the temple?

CHAPTER 16- BOWL JUDGMENTS

23. **(vs.1)** What instruction is given to the 7 angels?
24. **(vs.1)** Where did this voice come from?
25. **(vs.1)** What emotion of God is noted and acted upon by the 7 angels?

Tell what each bowl judgment is below and who it affects.

26. **(vs.2) BOWL 1-**
27. **(vs.3) BOWL 2-**
28. **(vs.4) BOWL 3-**
29. **(vs.5-7)** What praise does the angel give to God?
30. **(vs.6)** Why are earth dwellers worthy to receive this bowl judgment?
31. **(vs.8) BOWL 4-**
32. **(vs.9)** What was the response of the earth dwellers to bowl 4?
33. **(vs. 10) BOWL 5-**
34. **(vs.11)** Did the people repent of their deeds during bowl 5 judgment?
35. **(vs.12) BOWL 6-**
36. **(vs.13)** Out of whom did the 3 "frog"-like spirits come?
37. **(vs.14)** What is their purpose?
38. Think back to the church at Sardis (Revelation 3:3). What 4 things were they told to remember so they would be mindful of his return?

    1.
    2.
    3.
    4.

39. **(vs.15)** What blessing is given here?
40. **(vs.16)** Why is this bowl considered a judgment?
41. Read Isaiah 11:40-45. What is the first of Antichrist's military campaigns?
42. Read Zechariah 14:2. Where is the second siege?
43. **(vs.16)** What is the final battle?

44. **BOWL 7-**
45. **(vs.17)** What astounding pronouncement is given?
46. Read John 19:30. Who stated "It is finished?"
47. **(vs.18)** Do you remember where these voices, thunder and lightning have come from in our past readings?
48. **(vs.18-20)** Describe the earthquake and it's results.
49. **(vs.21)** What other occurrence was included in this bowl judgment?
50. **(vs.21)** How heavy was each hail stone?
51. **(vs.21)** What was man's response to this?

SPOILER: Mystery Babylon is about to be revealed!

What is **your** response to the seven bowl judgements?

REVELATION CHAPTERS 15 AND 16 ANSWER KEY

1. Seven angels with seven last plagues
2. They have the full wrath of God in them
3. It was mingled with fire
4. 1 Corinthians- We see through glass darkly now but in heaven we will see Him face to face clearly

   2 Corinthians- We constantly see the glory of the Lord changing us from glory to glory

   James- We read the Word and forget what we have seen if we are not applying what we have read to our works

5. Victory over the beast, Victory over his image, Victory over his Mark, Victory over the number of his name
6. Harps of God
7. The Song of Moses, The Servant of God
8. Redemption or Escape
9. Praise to Lord God Almighty for great and marvelous works, Just and true are his ways King of saints, He is holy
10. His judgements are made known
11. The tabernacle of the temple in heaven is open
12. Worshiping and testifying of God's greatness
13. 7
14. 7
15. Pure white linen and a golden girdle (chest covering)
16. The High Priest, Christ
17. The 4 "beasts" or 4 living creatures
18. Revelation 4:6
19. Living creatures, probably cherubim- see Ezekiel 10:15-20
20. Seven Golden Vials full of the wrath of God
21. Smoke from the glory of God and his power
22. Not until the 7 plagues of the 7 angels had been fulfilled
23. Go your ways and pour out vials of the anger of God on earth
24. Out of the temple
25. Anger/Wrath
26. Evil and grievous sore affecting those with the mark of the beast and who worship his image
27. The seas become like the blood of a dead man and every living thing in the sea dies
28. Rivers and fountains of water become blood
29. The Lord's judgement is righteous and true
30. They have shed the blood of the saints and prophets so they are judged in the same manner
31. The sun scorched the people with fire
32. They blasphemed God who had power over the plagues and did not repent
33. Darkness on the beast and his kingdom and the people gnawed their tongues due to pain
34. They blasphemed the God of heaven due to pain and sores and did not repent

35. The water of the Euphrates River dried up to prepare the way of the Kings of East
36. Out of the mouth of the Dragon (Satan), the Beast (Antichrist) and the False Prophet (Antichrist's Helper)
37. They are spirits of devils who do miracles happen to bring the whole world to battle of the great Day of the Lord Almighty
38. They were to remember what they had received and heard, to hold fast and repent
39. To watch and keep garments (righteousness) so they do not become ashamed
40. It is preparing the way for the Battle of Armageddon
41. Egypt
42. Jerusalem
43. Armageddon, Valley of Megiddo
44. Judgement on the air, voices come out of the temple, thunder, great earthquake
45. "It is done"
46. Jesus on the cross at his crucifixion
47. Revelation 4:5, Came from the throne and the 7 Spirits of God
48. Great, never before seen since creation, the city (either Jerusalem or Babylon) divided in 3 parts, cities of the nations fell, Babylon given the wine of the fierceness of his wrath, islands went away (sank) and the mountains flattened
49. Hail fell on man
50. 100 pounds
51. People blasphemed God because of the great plague of hail

REVELATION CHAPTERS 17 AND 18

BABYLON THE GREAT FALLS

WEEK 13

What are the origins of the city of Babylon and what do you think Babylon represents? Read Genesis 11:1-9 to capture some of the meaning before you begin this chapter.

1. **(vs.1)** Who told John to come here?
2. **(vs.1)** What was the angel going to show John?
3. **(vs.1)** Who is the great whore (or prostitute in some versions)? (Also see verse 5)
4. **(vs.2)** Who is the subject here?
5. **(vs.2)** What did they do that is mentioned here?
6. **Critical thinking**: What might this mean in today's times?
7. **(vs. 3)** Where did the angel carry John?
8. Who else went into the wilderness and why in Matthew 4:1-11?
9. **(vs.3)** On what color of beast is the woman sitting?
10. **(vs.3)** How many heads and horns does the beast have and what does this symbolism signify?
11. Who might this be referring to? (See Revelation 13:1.)
12. With what is scarlet often associated? (Isaiah 1:18)
13. **(vs.4)** Describe what the woman was wearing, (notice colors) and what does she have in her hand?
14. **(vs. 3 and 5)** What types of names are on the woman?
15. **(vs.5)** What is her title and where was it written?
16. What other references have we seen related to a symbol being on the forehead?
17. **(vs.6)** With what was the woman drunk?
18. Any thoughts on what this means?
19. **(vs.6)** What was John's response?
20. **(vs.7)** After this what help did the angel give John?
21. In contrast to this woman, who was the woman in Revelation 12?

Compare the two women:

Babylon-

Israel-

THE WOMAN AND THE BEAST EXPLAINED!

22. **(vs.8)** Where does the beast rise from?
23. **(vs.8)** Who is the beast and to where does he go?
24. From any source, look up the meaning of 'perdition'?
25. **(vs.8)** Who marveled at this beast?
26. **(vs.8)** Where did we see this "book of life" before in Revelation?
27. **(vs.9)** Who are the 7 heads according to verses 9 and 10?
28. **(vs.10)** This verse brings us back to the initial concept of Revelation in chapter 1, in which we see the things which John, the things that, and the things that . (Look this up in your first lesson).

Interesting facts:

According to the online Guzik Blue Letter Bible Commentary, vs. 10-11 are explained this way;

+'**5 fallen**' refers to 5 Empires before John's day :Egypt, Assyria, Babylonia, Medo-Persia and Greece

+'**one**' refers to the Roman Empire of John's day

+'**the other has not yet come**' refers to a one world Empire or a revived Roman Empire

29. **(vs.11)** It would naturally follow that the **eighth and future empire** would be that of who and He goes into where?
30. **(vs.12)** Who are the 10 horns, how long will they serve with the Antichrist, and what is their purpose? (Read Luke 22:53.)
31. **(vs.13)** What are the characteristics of the 10 kings?
32. **(vs.14)** With who do they try to make war?
33. **(vs.14)** Who overcomes and why?
34. **(vs.14)** What are the characteristics of 'those that are with him?
35. **(vs.15)** What four things does the water represent?
36. **(vs.16)** What response did the 10 horns have to the prostitute and what four things do the horns do?
37. **(vs.17)** Why do they do these things?
38. **(vs.17)** What will be the last thing that will stop all this action?
39. **(vs.18)** Who is the woman and what does she do?

CHAPTER 18

40. **(vs.1)** How did the earth respond to the next angel's power?
41. **(vs.2)** What did the angel say happened to Babylon and give his description?
42. **(vs.3)** What have the nations and kings done with Babylon?

43. **(vs.3)** What advantage do the merchants have with Babylon?
44. **(vs.4)** What strong warning is given to God's people? Why?
45. **(vs.5)** What response to Babylon does God have that is different from Christ's response to a sinner under the new covenant of salvation? (Read Hebrews 8:12.)
46. **(vs.6)** What is Babylon's reward?
47. **(vs.7-8)** What is the result of glorifying herself and living luxuriously?
48. **(vs.7)** What three boasts does Babylon say in her heart?
49. **(vs.8)** What is the result of these boasts? Why?
50. **(vs.9)** Why do the kings of the earth weep over her?
51. **(vs.10)** Are they living close by her now? Why?
52. **(vs.10)** What do they know about her judgment?
53. **(vs.11)** Why do the merchants weep?
54. **(vs.12-13)** List the merchandise they can no longer buy:
55. What categories of items do you see there? (Food, textiles, etc.)
56. **(vs.14)** What other things are gone?
57. **(vs.15)** Where are the merchants now? Why?
58. **(vs.16)** What are they remembering about Babylon?
59. **(vs.17)** How long does it take for her riches to come to an end?
60. **(vs.18)** What did the shipmasters, seafarer, sailors and business men cry?
61. **(vs.19)** What did they do in grief and what was their physical response?
62. **(vs.19)** Who became wealthy from Babylon here and once again, how long did destruction take?
63. **(vs.20)** Who is told to rejoice and why?
64. **(vs.21)** What did the angel throw in the sea?
65. **(vs.21)** How will Babylon be cast down and is it temporary?
66. Read Matthew 18:6 regarding another 'millstone' and what pronouncement is attached to it?
67. **(vs.22)** What musicians, artisans and sounds are silenced in Babylon?
68. **(vs.23)** What utility will be gone and what natural estate of man and woman will be gone?
69. **(vs.23)** What position did her merchants have there and how were all nations deceived by Babylon?
70. From any source, what is sorcery?
71. **(vs.24)** Whose blood was found in Babylon?

SPOILER: CHRIST IS COMING FOR A SECOND TOUCHDOWN ON THE EARTH!

What new thoughts about Babylon occurred to you in this section of Revelation?

REVELATION 17-18 ANSWER KEY

Babylonian origin is Tower of Babel. Man wanted to have life his own way and God separated language. Babylon represents current world political, monetary and world system and rebellion toward God.

1. One of the seven angels who had one of the seven vials showing continuation of the previous judgements
2. Judgement of the great prostitute which sits on many waters
3. Babylon- false world systems (religion, political systems, etc.
4. Kings of the earth, inhabitants of the earth
5. Committed fornication with Babylon, inhabitants drunk with the wine of her fornication
6. Being in love with false religion, money and world politics, being a globalist, one world government
7. Into the wilderness
8. Jesus, To face the temptation of Satan
9. Scarlet
10. Seven heads, Ten Horns, Allegiance in 10 ruling nations to a world ruler
11. Antichrist
12. Sin
13. Clothed in purple and scarlet, gold, precious stones, pearls, holding a golden cup of abominations and filthiness her fornication
14. Blasphemous names
15. On her forehead is written Mystery Babylon the Great, The Mother of Harlots and Abominations of the Earth
16. Revelation 7:3-4 – 144,000 sealed, Revelation 14:1 – Marked believers standing sealed with Lamb, Revelation 13:16 – Mark of the Beast on hand or forehead
17. Blood of the saints and martyrs
18. The world system is opposed to true faith in Christ and will be annihilating saints and martyring people.
19. He had great wonder toward this system
20. Told John he would explain the mystery of the beast with 7 heads and 10 horns carrying the woman 21. The woman in Revelation 12 is Israel
21. Babylon- Clothed in scarlet (sin) and purple, sitting on Antichrist, hand full of abomination, blood-drunk
    Israel-Clothed with the sun, moon under her feet, 12 star crown on her head, delivers man child-Christ
22. The bottomless pit
23. Antichrist, Perdition or eternal destruction
24. State of final spiritual ruin, soul loss – Dictionary.reference.com
25. Earth-dwellers whose names were not written in the book of life from the foundation of the world
26. Revelation 3:5, 13:8 (although this reference is "the book of life of the Lamb slain from the foundation of the world)

27. Seven mountains on which the woman sits (open to many interpretations; some say Rome which is synonymous with the Catholic Church, but it is some semblance of seven kings to begin with).
28. Saw, are currently, will come
29. Antichrist, into destruction
30. Ten horns are 10 kings, Serve "one hour" with the Antichrist, Purpose is to spread evil darkness
31. They have one mind and they give their cumulative power and strength to the Antichrist
32. The Lamb
33. The Lamb prevails because he is Lord of Lords and King of Kings
34. Called (their destiny), chosen (purpose), faithful (character)
35. People, multitudes, nations, tongues
36. Hate her, make her desolate and naked, eat her flesh and burn her with fire (Political power will overthrow the false church at this point, possibly mid-point in the Tribulation time).
37. God put it into their hearts to fulfil his will
38. God's word will be fulfilled
39. Great city which reigns over the kings of the earth, either Jerusalem (See Zechariah 14:4) or Babylon (See Revelation 18:2)
40. Light!
41. Fallen, Fallen, is a habitation of devils, every foul spirit, cage for unclean and hateful birds
42. Become drunk of the wine of the anger of her fornication, and fornicated with her
43. The merchants are rich with her delicacies
44. Come out of her and don't be partakers of her sin, so you don't receive her plagues
45. God remembers her sin whereas Christ remembers a redeemed persons sins no more
46. Double according to her works
47. Torment and sorrow
48. I am a queen, I am not a widow, I will not see sorrow
49. Her plagues come in one day with death, mourning, famine, burnt with fire, God is a strong judge
50. They see the smoke of her burning
51. They are far off, For fear of her torment
52. Judgement came in one hour
53. No man buys her merchandise anymore
54. Gold, silver, precious stones, pearls, linen, purple and silk, scarlet, wood, ivory, precious wood, brass, iron, marble, cinnamon, perfumes, ointments, frankincense, wine, oil, flour, wheat, beasts, sheep, horses, chariots, slaves, souls of men
55. Precious metals, textiles, building materials, industrial metals, luxuries, foods, farm animals, transportation, servants, the very souls of men
56. Fruits, dainty and refined things
57. Standing far from her, they fear her torment
58. Her fine linen and purple and scarlet clothes, gold, precious stones and pearls
59. One hour
60. "What city is like this great city?"
61. They put dust on their heads, They mourn, weep, and wail
62. All sea merchants were rich from her, In one hour she was desolate
63. Heaven, holy apostles and prophets, God avenged Babylon for them

64. A great millstone
65. With violence, It is permanent
66. Better to have a millstone around your neck and be cast into the sea then to offend a young believer
67. Harpists, musicians, pipers, trumpeters, sound of a millstone (no machinery)
68. Light, Marriage vows and celebrations
69. Merchants were great men of the earth, Nations were deceived by sorceries
70. Art of practicing spells by using supernatural powers through evil spirits per Websters.com
71. Prophets, Saints, all those that were slain on the earth

REVELATION CHAPTERS 19 AND 20

CHRIST'S SECOND COMING,
JUDGEMENT AND SATAN'S END

WEEK 14

Review from week 13. Which entity was destroyed in last week's lesson?

1. **(vs.1)** What five praises does this large group of people give the Lord?
2. **(vs.2)** What characterizes God's judgements?
3. **(vs.2)** Who did he judge and why did he do this?
4. **(vs.2)** What did God avenge?
5. From any source, what is the meaning of 'alleluia'?
6. **(vs.3)** Whose smoke rises up forever?
7. **(vs.4)** What praise do the 24 elders and the four beasts give God?
8. From any source, what is the meaning of 'amen'?
9. **(vs.5)** When the command comes out of the throne to "praise God", is there any respect of class, personage or rank?
10. **(vs.6)** What did the voice sound like?
11. **(vs.6)** Where did we see these descriptions before?
12. **(vs.6)** What praise did they give God here?
13. **(vs.7)** Why where they going to be glad, rejoice and give God honor?
14. **(vs.7)** Who is the "wife" here?
15. Look up the following references to wife/bride. Tell the subject of each.

Isaiah 61:10

Jeremiah 2:32

Revelation 21:2

Revelation 21:9-11

16. **(vs.8)** How is she to be dressed?
17. **(vs.8)** What does this clothing signify?
18. **(vs.9)** How is one invited to the marriage supper of the Lamb?
19. In Matthew 5:3-11 what blessings are given?
20. **(vs.9)** Who is the groom in vs 9?
21. **(vs.9)** What did the angel say about "the sayings of God"?
22. **(vs.10)** When John fell at his feet, why did the angel tell John not to worship him?
23. **(vs.10)** Who did he tell John to worship and why?
24. What does "the testimony of Jesus is the spirit of prophecy" mean? (Read Matthew 5:17)
25. **(vs.11)** What color horse does John see?
26. **(vs.11)** Think back to Revelation 6:2, the first Seal Judgement. Who was riding that white horse and what differences do you see in the two riders?
27. Who do we know is "faithful and true"? Read John 14:6, Deuteronomy 7:9, 1Corinthians 1:9, 10:13,

    2 Thessalonians 3:3, 1 Peter 4:19.

28. **(vs.11)** What does he do in righteousness?
29. **(vs.12)** Describe his eyes and what is on his head?
30. **(vs.12)** What is significant about his name?
31. Where in Revelation have we seen this before?
32. **(vs.13)** What was he clothed in and what is his name?
33. **(vs.14)** Describe his army.
34. Who else is clothed in fine linen in verse 8? (See questions 15 and 16 above)
35. **(vs.15)** What is in his mouth and of what is this significant? (See Hebrews 4:12)
36. **(vs.15)** What will he do with the sword and what does this mean?
37. **(vs.15)** How does he rule the nations?
38. Is this loving?
39. **(vs.15)** What is the purpose of Jesus walking on the grapes in the winepress of God Almighty?
40. **(vs.16)** What is written on his clothes and his thigh?
41. **(vs.17 &18)** What did the angel in the sun yell to the birds and what will they eat?
42. **(vs.19)** Who was going to make war against Jesus and his army?
43. **(vs.20)** From this verse who can we assume won the battle?
44. **(vs.20)** What is the disposition of the beast and the false prophet?
45. **(vs.20)** Those who received the mark of the beast and worshipped his image (the remnant) were judged by Jesus. How did he kill them and what happened to their bodies?

CHAPTER 20
SATAN IS BOUND

46. **(vs.1)** What does the angel have?
47. **(vs.2)** Who did he grab and why?

48. **(vs.3)** What is Satan's disposition and why is this done?

49. **(vs.3)** What other word is given to "the 1,000 years"?

50. **(vs.3)** How long is Satan released after the 1,000 years?

51. **(vs.4)** What two things did John see?

52. **(vs.4)** What purpose was given to them on the throne?

53. **(vs.4)** Give a description of the souls of those beheaded for the witness of Jesus and for the word of God; and what was their reward for this behavior?

54. **(vs.5)** What is the first resurrection?

55. **(vs.6))** Who is blessed and holy?

56. **(vs.6)** What honors and privilege do these people have?

57. **(vs.7)** Who is released from his prison after 1,000 years?

58. **(vs.8)** What is his plan?

59. **(vs.8)** Who are Gog and Magog and how many were in his army? (See Ezekiel 38:2-4)

60. **(vs.9)** What battle plan did they have?

61. **(vs.9)** What was God's swift and decisive response?

62. **(vs.10)** What is mentioned about what the devil did?

63. **(vs.10)** What happens to the devil, the beast and the false prophet (the unholy trinity)?

GREAT WHITE THRONE JUDGEMENT OF GOD ALMIGHTY

64. **(vs.11)** What did the earth and heaven do when they saw the occupant of the great white throne?

65. **(vs.12)** Who was standing before God?

66. **(vs.12)** What was opened? (See Daniel 7)

67. **(vs.12)** How were the unbelieving dead judged?

68. **(vs.13)** Which 3 places gave up the dead in them for judgement?

69. **(vs.13)** How were they judged?

70. **(vs.14)** What is the second death?

71. **(vs.15)** Who was cast into the lake of fire?

SPOILER: THE NEW JERUSALEM, A NEW HEAVEN AND A NEW EARTH ARE DESCRIBED IN DETAIL!

What did you learn that was new or interesting to you this lesson?

REVELATION 19 AND 20 ANSWER KEY

Review: Babylon

1. Alleluia, Salvation, Glory, Honor, Power
2. Truth and righteousness
3. The great prostitute, she corrupted the earth with her fornication
4. The blood of his servants on her hands
5. An exhortation to praise
6. Babylon
7. "Amen and Alleluia"
8. So be it truly
9. No, all his servants and them that fear God, both small and great
10. The sound of a great many people, many water, mighty thunderings
11. Revelation 1:15, 6:1, 19:1
12. "Alleluia: for the Lord God omnipotent reigns"
13. The marriage of the Lamb has come and his wife has made herself ready
14. The believer in Jesus Christ (the Lamb)
15. Clothing of salvation, righteousness, Bridal clothing, Bridal adornment, Beauty of New Jerusalem
16. Fine linen, clean and white
17. Righteousness of the Saints
18. They are called to this blessing
19. Poor in spirit will have the kingdom of heaven, Mourners will be comforted, Meek will inherit the earth, Those who hunger and thirst for righteousness will be filled, Merciful will obtain mercy, Pure in heart shall see God, Peacemakers will be called the children of God, Persecuted for righteousness sake shall have the kingdom of heaven, Those reviled and persecuted and spoken evil of will have great reward in heaven
20. The Lamb, Jesus
21. "These are the true sayings of God".
22. Don't do that. I am a fellow servant of your brothers who have the testimony of Jesus
23. Worship God, for the testimony of Jesus is the spirit of prophecy
24. Jesus showed himself as Savior to the world and is the fulfillment of all Bible prophecy
25. White
26. In 6:2, A bow and crown is given to him as he went out conquering with that is his motive, In 19:11 he is called Faithful and True and in righteousness he judges and makes war, His motive is righteousness.
27. Jesus, Faithful God, Lord, Creator
28. Judges and makes war
29. His eyes were like flames of fire and he had many crowns on his head
30. No one knows his name but He himself
31. Revelation 2:17-a white stone with a secret name for overcomers, 3:12-overcomer will have a new name written on him
32. He has a vesture dipped in blood, His name is 'The Word of God'

33. Heavenly armies followed Him on white horses, clothed in fine linen white and clean
34. The Bride of Christ, The believers in Jesus
35. Sharp sword, The Word of God
36. He will strike the nations, He is going to judge the nations of mankind
37. With a rod of iron
38. Not loving but just
39. Judgement and the justice of God is about to be meted out to the unbelieving world
40. KING OF KINGS AND LORD OF LORDS
41. Gather for the supper of the great God, The flesh of king, captains, mighty men, horses and riders, the flesh of all men, free and slave, small and great
42. The beast, the kings of the earth and their armies
43. Jesus
44. They are thrown into the lake of fire burning with brimstone
45. They were slain by the sword which came from his mouth (The Word of God), The birds at their flesh
46. The key of the bottomless pit and a great chain
47. Satan, the Devil, the old serpent, the dragon
48. Cast into the bottomless pit with a seal on him, So he will not deceive the nations until after the 1,000 years are completed
49. Millennium
50. A short season
51. Thrones, The souls of the beheaded
52. To judge
53. They did not worship the beast or his image and did not receive his mark on their forehead or hand, They lived and reigned with Christ 1,000 years
54. When the righteous are resurrected with their bodies before the Millennial reign of Christ
55. Those who have part in the first resurrection
56. The second death has no power over them, They shall be priest of God and Christ and reign with him a thousand years
57. Satan
58. Go out of prison to deceive the nations on the four quarters of the earth, gather Gog and Magog to battle
59. Enemies of God and some surmise they are the kingdoms of the North
60. To surround the camp of the saints and the beloved city (Jerusalem or Zion- see Psalm 87:2)
61. Fire came from God out of heaven and devoured them
62. He deceived the people
63. He is cast into the lake of fire and brimstone with the beast and the false prophet to be tormented day and night for ever and ever
64. The earth and the heaven "fled away"
65. The dead, small and great
66. The books and another book of life
67. They are judged by their works written in the books, Judged by the law if they did not receive God's grace through Christ's death on the cross for them

68. The sea, death and hell
69. They were judged every man according to his works
70. When death and hell are cast into the eternal lake of fire
71. Whoever was not found written in the book of life

REVELATION CHAPTERS 21 AND 22

HEAVEN AND THE NEW JERUSALEM

WEEK 15

1. **(vs.1)** What did John see that was "new"?
2. **(vs.1)** Why were these things "new" and what did John notice at the end of the verse?
3. **(vs.2)** What did John see come down from God?
4. **(vs.2)** What word picture did John use to tell us what this looked like?
5. According to Hebrews 12:22, who lives in this city (also called 'Zion')?
6. **(vs.3)** What did the voice from heaven tell John to behold ?
7. **(vs.3)** What is said about God in this verse?
8. **(vs.4)** God shows great compassion for our suffering by doing what?
9. **(vs.4)** What four former things are gone here?
10. **(vs.5)** What did God say from the throne say?
11. **(vs.5)** Why did he tell John to "write" and what is God saying to us here?
12. **(vs.6)** What magnificent statement is given here and who does God reveal himself to be?
13. The names 'Alpha and Omega' are only used 4 times in the Bible (Revelation 1:8, 1:11, 21:6, 22:3). Why might they all be in the Book of Revelation?
14. **(vs.6)** Who in Revelation 7:17 leads people to the fountain of the waters of life?
15. **(vs.7)** What inheritance is given and what relationship is seen there?
16. If all the "former things have passed away" (vs.7), what "things" will be inherited?
17. **(vs.8)** What 8 characteristics are given in opposition to the 'overcomer' in vs. 7?
18. **(vs.8)** What is their destination?
19. From the last lesson, Revelation 20:11-15, give another description of the "second death".
20. **(vs.9)** Which angel spoke to John here and where did we see him before?
21. **(vs.9-10)** Who was the angel going to show John and who is it revealed to be?
22. **(vs.10)** In Matthew 4:8 and Luke 4:5, who tried to imitate a mountain top revelation to Jesus in the wilderness.
23. **(vs.11)** Why was the light of Jerusalem like a precious stone, jasper or crystal?
24. **(vs.12-13)** Describe the wall and gates and what is the division of the gates?
25. **(vs.14)** How many foundations are there and why?
26. **(vs.15)** Who is tasked with measuring the city, the gates and the walls?
27. **(vs.16)** What shape is the city and how long is 12,000 furlongs?

28. **(vs.17)** How wide is the wall at 144 cubits?

29. **(vs.18-21)** Give description of each part of the city below:

The wall:

The city:

The 12 foundations of precious stones in order are:

The 12 gates:

The city streets:

30. **(vs.22)** Who is now the temple in the New Jerusalem?
31. **(vs.23)** Who lights the city and how?
32. **(vs.24)** Who will walk in the light of the city and who will bring their glory and honor to it?
33. **(vs.25)** Do the gates ever shut? Explain.
34. **(vs.26)** What is brought into the city?
35. **(vs.27)** What three characteristics will never enter the city and who *is* allowed to enter?

CHAPTER 22

36. **(vs.1)** What is the significance of the river? (See Isaiah 48:18)
37. Read Psalm 46:4-5. What does the river do for the city of God?
38. What element on earth must we have to live? (From any source)
39. **(vs.2)** Where is the tree of life?
40. Where was the first tree of life? (See Genesis 3:22)
41. **(vs.2)** How many types of fruit are on the tree and what is it's cycle of producing?
42. **(vs.2)** What are the leaves used for and what does this lead you to believe?
43. **(vs.3)** What will be no more?
44. Which verses in Genesis 3 speak of the original curses (judgement) on mankind?
45. **(vs.3)** Who is in the city that will be served?
46. In Isa. 65:18-25 what city and people are being described?
47. **(vs.4)** What two honors are given to the servants of God?
48. **Personal reflection:** How does this impact you to know you will see Jesus' face?
49. Remembering back to Revelation 14:1, what name is on the foreheads of the 144,000?
50. **(vs.5)** What lights the reign of God's servants forever?
51. In John 8:12, who is the Light of the world?
52. What lesson should we learn about 'light' in 2 Corinthians 6:14?
53. **(vs.6)** What does the angel tell John about the nature of the revelation?
54. **(vs.6)** Who does the angel say sent him to the servant and why?
55. **(vs.7)** What proclamation and blessing are given and does your personal fellowship warrant this blessing?

56. **(vs.8)** What did John do a second time that he was told not to do earlier?
57. **(vs.9)** Who was he told to worship?
58. **(vs.10)** In contrast to Revelation 10:4 what is John told here?
59. Why is he told this?
60. **(vs.11)** What is being said to all mankind?
61. **(vs.12)** Who is coming with his rewards for each man's work?
62. What does James 2:20 say about this?
63. **(vs.13-17)** What parts of the Godhead is here?
64. **(vs.14)** What is the blessing and privilege here?
65. **(vs.15)** Who is outside the city?
66. **(vs.16)** Who does Jesus, (who sent the angel to the churches), claim to be?
67. **(vs.16)** Why do you think Jesus declares who he is here? (Read Jeremiah 23:5-6, Luke 1:32-33)
68. **(vs.17)** What do the "Spirit and the bride" say?
69. **(vs.17)** What does the hearer say?
70. **(vs.17)** What does the thirsty do?
71. **(vs.17) Personal reflection:** What is this verse about for the world today?
72. **(vs.18)** What will happen if a man hears the words of this prophecy but adds to it?
73. List a few plagues or judgements we learned about in Revelation:
74. **(vs.19)** If a man takes away from the prophecy of this book what 3 things are taken from him?
75. **(vs.19)** What three things does God take away in response to a person taking away from the words of the book of this prophecy?
76. **(vs.20)** He who testifies of these thing says what and how many times did he say this in chapter 22
77. What should our response to our Savior be?
78. **(vs.21)** What is given to us as a parting gift from the Lord?

What is your response to the King of the Universe after studying the Book of Revelation?

Are you ready to fully give your life to Jesus the Christ, the Light of the world, the Lion of the Tribe of Judah? Say this prayer: Lord Jesus, I confess I am a sinner in need of the forgiveness only you as Savior can give. Please forgive my sins. I cannot merit your grace apart from your death on the cross. Thank you for dying as the substitutionary sacrifice in my place and making me acceptable to God the Father. Please come into my life and be my King and God forever! Amen

Find a Bible believing church and seek out someone to disciple you in the Word of God.

THE END

COME QUICKLY LORD JESUS!

REVELATION 21 AND 22 ANSWER KEY

1. Heaven and earth
2. The first heaven and earth were destroyed, there was no more sea
3. The holy city of New Jerusalem
4. A bride prepared for her husband
5. The church age believers and the body of Christ
6. The tabernacle of God is with men
7. God himself will dwell with (and be with) them, they shall be his people, and He will be their God
8. He wipes away all tears from their eyes
9. Death, sorrow, crying, pain
10. "Look, I make all things new"
11. Because these words are true and faithful, God is revealing his character to mankind
12. "It is done", "I am Alpha and Omega, the beginning and the end
13. It starts and ends the book, All the information, laws, judgements, heavenly realms belong to God
14. Jesus
15. The overcomer inherits all things, The relationship is now as God to a son
16. One thing we know for sure is in Revelation 2:7, "to eat from the tree of life" in the middle of God's paradise, also in Revelation 21:6, to drink from the "fountain of the water of life freely"
17. Fearful, unbelieving, abominable, murderers, whoremonger (fornicators), sorcerers, idolaters, all liars
18. The lake that burns with fire and brimstone, The second death
19. Great white throne judgement where all unbelieving are judged, even sea gave up dead, Death and hell are thrown into the lake of fire
20. One of the 7 angels who had the 7 vials of the 7 last plagues, Revelation 15:7
21. The bride, the Lamb's wife
22. The devil
23. It has the glory of God as the light
24. Great high wall (massive), 12 gates having the names of the 12 tribes of Israel written thereon with 12 angels, one at each gate, Three gates one per side divided toward east, north, south, west
25. Twelve foundations named for the 12 apostles of the Lamb
26. One of the 7 angels who had the 7 vials of the 7 last plagues
27. An equal sided square (length=width), The Ryrie Study Bible notes say 12,000 is about 15,000 miles
28. The Ryrie Study Bible notes say 144 cubits is 216 feet wide
29. Wall of Jasper, City of pure gold clear like glass, Jasper, sapphire, chalcedony (greenish), emerald, sardonyx (red/white), sardius (bright red), chrysolyte (golden), beryl (sea green), topaz (yellow/green), chrysoprasus (apple green), jacinth (blue), amethyst (purple), 12 pearl gates of one large pearl, streets of gold clear like glass
30. The Lord God Almighty and the Lamb
31. There is no need for sun or moon to shine as God's glory and the Lamb are the light
32. The saved nations, the kings of the earth
33. Gates never shut because there is no night there

34. The glory and honor of the nations
35. Anything that defiles, works of abomination, lies, Those written in the Lamb's book of life
36. Peace like a river and righteousness as the waves of the sea, It was crystal clear coming from the throne of God
37. Makes glad the city of God
38. Water
39. In the middle of the street and on either side of the river
40. Within reach in the Garden of Eden
41. Twelve different types of fruit yielding fruit every month
42. For the healing of the nations, That the nations of the earth which were under the curse and judgement of God will progress to full healing in heaven
43. Curse
44. Verses 8-24, curse of the serpent, woman, man, ground
45. God and the Lamb (Jesus) will be served by God's servants
46. The New Jerusalem, God's elect people
47. We will see God's face, his name will be on their forehead
48. Personal reflection
49. God the Father's name
50. The Lord God's light
51. Jesus
52. Light and darkness cannot coexist
53. Everything he just heard is faithful and true
54. The Lord God of the Holy prophets, To show his servants the things which must quickly be done
55. "Look, I am coming quickly", Blessed is the one who keeps the Bible prophesy
56. Worshiped an angel
57. God
58. In 10:4 John was told to seal up the 7 thunders voices, but here was told not to seal the prophecy
59. The time is at hand for the prophecy of the Bible to be completed
60. No more chances for the grace of God, the unjust and filthy will remain so, the righteous and holy will also remain as their actions have been judged, "It is finished!"
61. Jesus
62. Faith without works is dead
63. The trinity, God the Father, Jesus and the Holy Spirit
64. Blessed are those who do his commandments, 2 rights or privileges: right to the tree of life, may enter through the gates of the city
65. The dogs, sorcerers, whoremongers, murderers, idolaters, those that love lying
66. The root and offspring of David, The bright and morning star
67. He is proclaiming his heritage and confirms his genealogy and true nature which is confirmed through Biblical prophecy
68. Come
69. Come
70. Comes, Reminds us we are currently in the age of God's grace and we can take of the water of life freely

71. Personal reflection
72. God will add the plagues in this book to his life
73. Seals, trumpets, bowl judgements, blood, famine, pestilence, signs in the earth and heaven
74. From him is taken his part out of the book of life, citizenship in the holy city and the things which are included in this book (blessings, inheritance, eternal life)
75. Taken out of the book of life, out of the holy city, and from the things written in this book
76. Says "Surely I come quickly", Three times (verses 7, 12, 20)
77. To be able to say, "Come quickly Lord Jesus!"
78. The grace of our Lord Jesus Christ is given to all

Printed in the United States
By Bookmasters